INSIDE THE COCKPIT

INSIDE THE COCKPIT

NAVIGATING THE COMPLEXITY OF DRUG DEVELOPMENT WITH AI AND BLOCKCHAIN

GUNJAN BHARDWAJ

LIONCREST
PUBLISHING

INSIDE THE COCKPIT
Navigating the Complexity of Drug
Development with AI and Blockchain

ISBN   978-1-5445-1309-6 *Paperback*
       978-1-5445-1308-9 *Ebook*

CONTENTS

INTRODUCTION

IN DECEMBER 2014, A TWENTY-NINE-YEAR-OLD investor named Vivek Ramaswamy bought a patent from GlaxoSmithKline (GSK) for $5 million. The patent covered an Alzheimer's drug candidate that had failed GSK's clinical testing. This isn't uncommon; in fact, most drug candidates fail (one study found that between 2006 and 2015 only 9.6 percent of drug development programs made it to market).[1] GSK, seeking to recoup some of its investment in what appeared to be a dead-end project, was more than willing to sell its intellectual property.

Ramaswamy knew something GSK didn't. He was eager to buy.

---

1   David W. Thomas, Justin Burns, John Audette, Adam Carroll, Corey Dow-Hygelund, and Michael Hay, *Clinical Development Success Rates 2006–2015* (Biotechnology Innovation Organization, Biomedtracker, and Amplion), 7, https://www.bio.org/sites/default/files/Clinical%20Development%20Success%20Rates%202006-2015%20-%20BIO,%20Biomedtracker,%20Amplion%202016.pdf.

Typically, drug testing involves a "stage gate" process characterized by multiple decision points, or stage gates, along the way. If a drug fails to meet performance requirements at any decision point (DP), development is stopped. Drugs like the one Ramaswamy bought, known as SB-742457, fill decision-point graves. GSK had conducted thirteen trials involving 1,250 patients before concluding at DP-02, or decision point two, that further study was unwarranted. In 2010, it abandoned SB-742457, evidently one more in a long line of failures that characterize the hunt for blockbuster drugs.

In early 2014, Ramaswamy, a hedge fund partner, had information that helped him understand something that the GSK researchers did not: SB-742457, taken with another Alzheimer's drug, Aricept, slowed cognitive decline for a certain subset of dementia patients. In May 2014, Ramaswamy left his hedge fund. Within eight months, he raised $360 million to launch his new company, Axovant Sciences, built around SB-742457. When Axovant went public in mid-2015, even though the firm had done no further clinical studies, the new company's market valuation topped $2 billion—based on a single $5 million purchase of a "failed" drug.[2]

---

2   "Did a 29-Year-Old Show GlaxoSmithKline That It Made a Billion Dollar Mistake?" PharmaCompass, June 25, 2015, https://www.pharmacompass.com/radio-compass-blog/did-a-29-year-old-show-glaxosmithkline-that-it-made-a-billion-dollar-mistake.

GSK had sold Ramaswamy a treasure for almost nothing.

He had taken advantage of the information asymmetry that's pervasive in the life sciences market. Companies like GSK often don't even know the value of what they have because they can't see a complete picture; data is scattered across the life sciences ecosystem in hidden pockets and walled gardens. Making connections and drawing insights from that data, consequently, is very difficult.

In order to understand the value of the data in the drug development value chain, it's crucial to understand the context, which is dauntingly complex. To obtain a view of the landscape in, say, Alzheimer's research, one would have to manually curate and annotate all the relevant research data, then look at the relationships within it. For most researchers today, this is essentially impossible. Companies that do this work employ armies of analysts and sell the results for a substantial premium. Big pharmaceutical firms may be able to pay for their research, which gives them a leg up in the hunt for blockbuster drugs (though no guarantee they'll be the only ones finding them, as Vivek Ramaswamy showed).

The result is information asymmetry, and the value of that asymmetry is growing exponentially, given the growth in the volume of life sciences data. In 1950, medical knowledge was believed to double every fifty years; by 2020, it is expected to double every seventy-three days.[3] Even at a huge pharma like GSK, they were—and are—sitting on an unexploited treasure trove in terms of the value of the research and development work. But they didn't know that in the case of SB-742457. They didn't know that the drug could be repurposed and used for a certain subset of patients. In all likelihood, they are sitting on other treasures they don't recognize because they are not able to glean the appropriate insights from the life sciences data landscape.

DRUG DEVELOPMENT IS BROKEN

Ramaswamy and GSK's experience is one example of what's broken in drug discovery and development. Data is hidden away in carefully protected silos, and that secrecy means that important discoveries are not happening at the pace at which they should.

This problem is not limited to big pharmaceutical companies; consider a story I heard from a research scientist at the University of Göttingen in Germany who works on the epigenetics of pancreatic cancer—one of the deadliest cancers in the world, a cancer with one of the lowest five-

---

3   Peter Densen, "Challenges and Opportunities Facing Medical Education," *Transactions of the American Clinical and Climatological Association* 122, (2011): 48–58, https://www.ncbi.nlm.nih.gov/pmc/articles/PMC3116346/.

year survival rates, less than 5 percent.[4] Many candidate drugs for treating pancreatic cancer have failed miserably. This scientist described a drug that was in clinical trials but had been abandoned because it failed to meet the safety and efficacy criteria of the US Food and Drug Administration (FDA). The reality was that this drug actually *cured* the tumor in a select subset of patients. If one were to look at the epigenetics of the drug's efficacy and stratify the patient population appropriately, it could be a wonder drug for a smaller segment of patients. But it wasn't being pursued.

Failed, or apparently failed, drug experiments go to the valley of death. During the period from 2013 to 2015, 218 drugs failed at Stage II or Stage III trials.[5] The decision has been made by their creators that they are not worth pursuing, yet valuable data is locked up in those experiments. That data still is useful. Some researcher somewhere, if he had that data, might see a connection to something that otherwise seems unrelated, and see possibility, just as Vivek Ramaswamy did. Instead, the data about those failed experiments is not published, not searchable, and not available—no one can even find out

---

4   Boris W. Kuvshinoff and Mark P. Bryer, "Treatment of Respectable and Locally Advanced Pancreatic Cancer," *Cancer Control* 7, no. 5 (2000): 428 & ff, https://moffitt.org/File%20 Library/Main%20Nav/Research%20and%20Clinical%20Trials/Cancer%20Control%20 Journal/v7n5/428.pdf.

5   Richard K. Harrison, "Phase II and Phase III Failures: 2013–2015," *Nature Reviews* 15 (2016): 817–818, http://www.whartonwrds.com/wp-content/uploads/2017/11/Nature-Paper-Richard_ Harrison Phase-II-Phase-III-Failure-Rates pdf

that a researcher conducted an experiment. Researchers only want to publish what seems to work, yet a broader understanding of what doesn't work can also be useful in the search for drugs.

Big Pharma companies might be holding hidden treasures, but they can't get a real-time look at the entire gamut of drug candidates and the intellectual property (IP) of those candidates. They can't combine their own research with outside research to come up with drugs that will help patients, which of course is why pharmaceutical companies should exist. The direct advantage of looking at the entire research universe, internal and external, is that researchers can see insights and correlations that they could not previously see when data was trapped in silos. The present system of siloing data and information asymmetry characterizes the life sciences ecosystem and hampers the discovery of potentially lifesaving drugs.

The example of SB-742457 illustrates how broken our system of drug discovery and development actually is. Every day, people suffer and die because life sciences and pharmaceutical industries don't have the technologies and capabilities they should and could have to bring effective drugs to market more quickly and effectively.

Drug discovery is hampered by a structural system that resembles driving a car by looking in the rearview mirror.

Imagine a physician sitting in the cockpit of a race car. What is flying against his windshield is not wind, but data—the whole life sciences data universe. If the physician wants to drive fast and safely and get where he intends to go, he drives by looking out the windshield. But in life sciences, we drive the car by looking in the rearview mirror—that is, we look at historical data. Worse, we don't even look at *recent* historical data; we look at *old* historical data. It's as if there's a time delay for what we're seeing in our car's rearview mirror.

Because insights about that data are manually curated and delayed by the process of scientific publication, we are not able to see the data in real time. Peer review of publishable data takes up to 250 days, and the time lag from completion of research to publication can be a year.[6] That's why GSK sold Axovant a promising Alzheimer's drug for a pittance; the firm's researchers were not able to see what the extant, current research on Alzheimer's looks like.

Ramaswamy and Axovant were able to get a glimpse through the windshield, and that glimpse was worth $2 billion.

---

6   C.H.J. Hartgerink, "Publication Cycle: A Study of the Public Library of
    Science (PLOS)," Authorea, https://www.authorea.com/users/2013/
    articles/36067 publication cycle a study of the public library of science plos/_chow_article.

THE SYSTEM IS STRUCTURALLY FLAWED

Drug discovery and development are crippled by a three-fold structural problem.

First, insights are not real-time. We drive the drug-discovery car while looking at data in the time-delayed rearview mirror. By the time you see something, you're actually well beyond the moment when the researcher who did the work understood it. In life sciences, this delay is a result of slow publication of research data, even as the pace of drug research speeds up. Those delays limit insights.

Second, there is enormous information asymmetry in the life sciences universe. Some researchers and treatment centers have greater access to data and insights because they can afford to pay for it. Many small and medium biotech companies and smaller treatment companies, not to mention patients, have little or no access to these insights. The data is not democratized, which means fewer opportunities for researchers to work with the data.

Third, there is substantial innovation redundancy. In an efficient drug-discovery ecosystem, researchers know what other researchers are doing. Novelty requires competition, but competition doesn't mean five people should conduct the same experiment that five others did before them. If someone conducted the experiment and the hypothesis that the researcher tested was not proven, why should others repeat that research to get the same results? Yet this happens because one of the principal currencies in science is not solving health problems—it's publication credits that build reputation. The way science operates, researchers are rewarded with prestige, credentials, grant money, and other benefits when they are the first to publish a finding in a respected scientific journal. Researchers publish positive findings—not proof of a null hypothesis. No one is interested in learning about what didn't work; they want to learn about what did work. They don't publish data about proving the null hypothesis, and they don't discuss their work until after publication. In fact, researchers are disincentivized to share their research or findings prior to publication. A German researcher at the University of Göttingen told me that this kind of competition leads to some researchers attending scientific congresses for the purposes of seeking to understand others' current research projects and trying to rush their own competing work into publication first.

Think about that for a moment; think about how *wrong* that is. We live in an era when the public political narrative labels Big Pharma as "evil," as nothing more than faceless corporations that only care about profits, not patients. Yet if that's the case, then scientists are evil, too, because what they care about is getting published first, rather than helping patients. These perspectives are caricatures; of course scientists want to help patients. From the outside, the behaviors of Big Pharma companies and researchers may seem to be focused on other objectives, but they make more sense when we comprehend the underlying incentives. The way the system is built now, they have to achieve those objectives if they are going to help patients. A company that didn't care about profits likely wouldn't survive long enough to do meaningful work, and a researcher who was ineffective at gaining publication credits would not be able to continue his work.

Step back and look at this situation: who would create a system of drug discovery that actively disincentivizes the people working in the business from cooperating with each other? If, for example, you truly wanted to help people who are suffering from pancreatic cancer, why wouldn't you want everyone who is working on pancreatic cancer, from a doctor treating patients in a rural clinic to the world's largest drug manufacturers, to be communicating and cooperating with each other?

That's not the system that exists right now. But it could be.

Right now, the incentives in the drug-discovery ecosystem are misaligned. Society wants drugs that cure diseases. Scientists want to publish original findings.

Pharmaceutical companies want blockbuster drugs worth $1 billion or more.

I wrote this book to introduce a new paradigm for drug discovery: a way of ordering the life sciences ecosystem that relies on artificial intelligence (AI) and blockchain technologies to change incentives and enable faster discovery of more-effective drugs.

In the following chapters, I will describe what this ecosystem looks like and how it is already coming into being. As I described above, three primary problems limit drug discovery: lack of real-time information; information asymmetry; and innovation redundancy. The new paradigm is built on three major changes to the current system to address those problems:

The first change is real-time access to data. Researchers will be able to look forward out the windshield of their cockpit at the data universe, rather than continuing to drive toward drug discovery by looking in the rearview mirror.

The second change is sharing data to create large data training sets for artificial intelligence. This creates economies of scale and economies of scope, allowing AI to be brought to bear in the hunt for drugs. Artificial intelligence can be used not only to look at the data to evaluate researchers' hypotheses; it also can develop previously unconsidered hypotheses and evaluate these.

The third change is to stop restricting access to critical data through data privacy laws. Rather than limiting access to data, as is the current trend, I will show how patients, researchers, and institutions can be incentivized to share health data and yet also retain their privacy using blockchain technology.

CHANGE IS A MORAL IMPERATIVE

Drug development is a complex business. Pharmaceutical companies spend decades and billions of dollars to bring drugs onto the market. In 2016, the top ten pharmas spent a combined $70.5 billion on R&D.[7] Between 2010 and 2013, the US Food and Drug Administration reduced the average approval time on oncology drugs by 4 percent—and it still takes 9.8 years to get a drug approved. This reality pushes drug companies to work in the most potentially lucrative areas, such as oncology and neurodegenerative diseases, because they need a lot of financial headroom if they are to recoup enormous development costs. Research in rare diseases (those suffered by 200,000 individuals or fewer) sees much less

---

7   Ben Adams, "The Top 10 Pharma R&D Budgets in 2016," FiercePharma, https://pages.
      questexweb.com/rs/294-MQF-056/images/The%20top%2010%20pharma%20R%26D%20
      budgets%20in%202016%20REV2.pdf

investment, even though an estimated 350 million people worldwide are afflicted with one or more of the two thousand identified rare diseases.[8]

We should challenge the current drug discovery and development paradigm not because drug companies are evil, but because the system is slow and inefficient, and that is morally wrong. The current structure limits the ability of researchers to address all diseases, leading them to focus on the most profitable. We should be doing everything we can to get lifesaving drugs to the people who need them sooner, and one way to do that is to reduce the cost of drug discovery. When drugs are less expensive to develop, the opportunity to profitably investigate rare diseases expands. Morality demands it.

This work isn't just a professional imperative for me; it's a personal one. In 2010, a close friend and mentor in Frankfurt called me late at night to share the devasting news that he had been diagnosed with cancer. The following days were frustrating. I spent hours with him in the hospital, asking, "Why do you believe this doctor? Why do you believe what he says? Is there a way we could do research ourselves on these tumor types to find out about alternative therapies? Who are the key leaders in this field we can ask for second opinions?"

---

8   "Investment in Research Saves Lives and Money," Research America, https://www.
     researchamerica.org/sites/default/files/Rare%20Diseases%20Fact%20Sheet_2015.pdf

It was impossible. There was just no way to understand whether he was truly getting the best advice or the best treatment, based on his specific disease pattern.

I was very frustrated, and when I spoke to my father about it, he said, "Don't complain. Change." This is not the typical advice of a middle-class Indian father. Most want their children to follow a safe, secure career path. Although I had started several companies early in my career, I had settled onto that path. I was working as a consultant with Boston Consulting Group, where I had been a manager for two years and had a global program budget. I was on a secure track.

"Start," my father said.

I understood what was wrong with the way we seek cures for disease. I had ideas about how to change things. My mother was very concerned that I was making a mistake, but I knew my purpose was right.

My vision was, and remains, this: any patient, anywhere, scared and facing a terrifying diagnosis, will know that the treatment being offered is the best available. That person will have the best chance to come through alive, not to relapse, and to live a rich life.

I knew I could make a difference if I could create a system

that would enable those situations. I have started two companies, Innoplexus in Germany and CancerCoin in Switzerland, that do just this. This book is not intended to champion these companies. Rather, I am writing in order to share my vision and the progress that is being made toward that vision.

The paradigm is already changing. The combination of AI and blockchain technologies is fundamentally altering the way the life sciences ecosystem operates, creating new pathways for the discovery of lifesaving drugs. In the following pages, I will show you how.

CHAPTER 1

THE PAIN OF DRUG DISCOVERY

ONE OF MY COLLEAGUES, A BOARD MEMBER OF OUR company, called me one day in 2017 with a very serious problem. A friend's wife had been diagnosed with stage 3 breast cancer. It had metastasized into her body, and she had begun chemotherapy. The chemo had been ineffective, so she was put in an immunotherapy trial program. Because it was a trial, she didn't know if she was receiving the immunotherapy or a placebo.

Her condition worsened to the point that her doctors, for ethical reasons, revealed that she had been given a placebo. She was in dire straits.

"What are the alternatives?" my colleague asked me. "Which other physicians can provide a second opinion?

In what European medical centers are they conducting studies for similar conditions? Who are the top European oncologists we can speak to who might have different treatment ideas?"

My colleague was concerned. His friend was anguished. His friend's wife was dying.

Part of the work we do at Innoplexus is designed to answer exactly these kinds of questions. We build systems that show the entire research landscape for various diseases and treatment modalities. Because of this, I did know someone to talk to. I knew of a targeted therapy that was in trials at a Big Pharma company, and I strongly recommended it.

A few months later, I met the woman in question at a party in Vienna. "Gunjan," she said, "it's really great! There are very few side effects. I feel way better, and this drug has done wonders for me." She was effusive in her thanks.

I was glad we could help her. But I was saddened, too, that she received our help only because she was a woman in a Western country whose husband happened to know the right people. Her story was a personal triumph over certain death, but it was also a stark illustration of one of the core structural problems of drug discovery and development today.

What about that patient with that same cancer in a clinic in rural Texas? Or in Rajasthan? In America or Europe, a cancer diagnosis is scary, but at least patients there have access to the latest effective medicine.

In the developing world, where there is even less access to effective treatment, the word "cancer" is treated like a death sentence. Usually, in those places, where a patient may not even have a bed and has to take chemo sitting on the ground outside a treatment center, it is. Mortality rates in developed countries are lower, despite higher incidence rates, because of the availability of quality diagnosis and treatment services.[1] Don't each of those patients deserve the same shot at a long, full life as a socially connected woman in Austria?

THREE IMPEDIMENTS

Drug innovation and development takes too long and costs too much for three reasons.

The first is the inherently fuzzy nature of innovation, a magical buzzword that requires the marriage of structure

---

1   Miriam López-Gómez, Eduardo Malmierca, Miguelde Górgolas, and Enrique Casado, "Cancer in Developing Countries: The Next Most Preventable Pandemic," *Critical Reviews in Oncology/Hematology* 88, no. 1 (2013): 117–122, https://www.croh-online.com/article/S1040-8428(13)00071-1/pdf; "10 Must-Know 2015 Global Cancer Facts," American Cancer Society, February 4, 2015, https://www.cancer.org/latest-news/10-must-know-2015-global-cancer-facts.html.

and creativity in order to occur. In the drug development world, it's a long process.

Innovation begins with having a large number of ideas—everything you dump into the top of the innovation funnel. Drug development begins with as many as ten thousand ideas to produce a single commercially viable drug. If you lack large numbers of ideas, your chances of success plummet. Simply generating that volume of innovation is an impediment.

The second limit on innovation is the throughput rate. How fast are these ideas run through the innovation funnel, either to be abandoned or to move forward? The faster you can move ideas through, the more money you save. Cutting a month off the clinical testing for candidate drugs can save millions of dollars and earn millions of dollars too.

The savings fact is intuitive—the earning aspect, less so. Here's what I mean. Drugs face what's called a "patent cliff": that moment, usually twenty years after a patent was filed, when the generic drug manufacturers can begin making a competing drug. Once you hit the patent cliff, your market share drops by 85 or 90 percent. Generic drugs tend to be priced 80 to 85 percent lower than the original, patented drugs.[2]

---

2   Allison Gilchrist, "5 Drug Spending Trends to Watch," *Pharmacy Times*, April 26, 2016, https://www.pharmacytimes.com/news/5-drug-spending-trends-to-watch.

Drug companies file for patents when they begin clinical testing on drugs, and that starts the clock ticking. They have twenty years to recoup their investment and make a profit. Every month they spend on the market, rather than still in testing, is another month in that twenty-year time frame devoted to making money. A faster throughput rate translates into greater profitability. Lower throughput rates limit the commercial viability of candidate drugs.

The third limit on innovation is variability of ideas. If your ten thousand ideas come from a similar source, the odds of having a successful drug at the end of the process are low. You don't simply need many ideas—you need many *different* ideas. You achieve different ideas by differentiating the creators of those ideas.

There is a concept in science called "minimum requisite variability of a system." That means that the variability of the system that is controlling the inside of the system (the drug-discovery process) should be similar to the variability outside of the system (the patient and diagnosis universe). For example, if you are building a product for a diverse set of buyers, such as a car, you should have a diverse set of designers that reflects those buyers. A similar idea applies in drug development. You want a high degree of cognitive variability, which means seeking ideas from a development team that comes from different backgrounds, different types of education, and so on.

Healthy innovation is predicated on an ecosystem that can source ideas in this way.

WHY DRUG DEVELOPMENT TAKES SO LONG

Discovery, development, and approval of new drugs is a laborious and expensive process that takes roughly a decade. Interestingly, FDA approval times of drugs that have completed clinical trials have dropped substantially since 1980, yet the journey to a successful drug remains a long one.[3]

LABORATORY RESEARCH AND DEVELOPMENT: THREE TO SIX YEARS

The process begins with target identification. What will the drug do? Researchers must understand the processes or pathways by which a drug will deliver the effect they want. Then they identify five thousand to ten thousand laboratory compounds, which they screen in laboratories to determine, first, if they have the ability to affect the identified target, and second, if they interfere with other related targets. In this way, researchers identify which compounds are most promising. This preliminary

---

3   Daniel Carpenter, Michael Chernew, Dean G. Smith, and A. Mark Fendrick, "Approval Times for New Drugs: Does the Source of Funding for FDA Staff Matter?" *Health Affairs*, December 17, 2003, 619 & ff., https://www.pharmamedtechbi.com/~/media/Images/Publications/Archive/The%20Pink%20Sheet/65/051/00650510017/031222_fda_funding_study.pdf.

process takes three to six years and produces about 250 candidate drugs.

PRECLINICAL STUDIES: ONE YEAR

Next come in vitro ("in glass") studies of the effect of the molecules on cells in test tubes. Those that look promising are moved along to in vivo ("in the living") studies in animals. Researchers test for toxicity, efficacy, and how quickly the drug is processed by the body.

The candidates that continue to show potential advance through at least two mammalian studies (only one may involve rodents) to test further for toxicity. Approximately five candidate drugs of the original ten thousand make it this far.

CLINICAL TRIALS: FOUR TO SEVEN YEARS

Clinical trials, which involve human volunteers, go through three phases. Phase I trials test side effects and how quickly drugs are absorbed and excreted. These are small trials, usually involving between twenty and eighty people. About 70 percent of drugs move past this phase.

Phase II trials involved one hundred to three hundred people who have the condition the drug is designed to target. This phase tests the drug's efficacy. Some patients are given the drug; some are given a placebo. One-third of remaining drug candidates clear this hurdle.

Phase III trials involve one thousand to three thousand patients. Here the drug is tested to compare its efficacy against other treatments, its interaction with other drugs, and different dosages. If all goes well, a single winning drug is identified.

REVIEW AND APPROVAL: ONE TO TWO YEARS

We estimate that one drug makes it this far for every five thousand to ten thousand candidates.[4] [5] Even then, it may not make it to market. A regulatory body, such as the United States Food and Drug Administration, reviews everything that has gone into testing the drug, focusing on safety and efficacy. If the benefits of the drug are deemed to supersede the risks, the drug will be approved. But one in four drugs at this point, so close to the wire, is rejected.

Throughout this entire process, the Big Pharma or bio-tech firm working on developing the drug continues to evaluate it in a parallel program that assesses not only

---

4   Ding, Man et al., eds., *Innovation and Marketing in the Pharmaceutical Industry: Emerging Practices, Research and Policies*, Springer Science and Business Media, New York, 2014

5   Fitzgerald, Gerald A., "Re-engineering Drug Discovery and Development," *LDI Issue Brief*, Leonard Davis Institute of Health Economics, Vol. 17, Issue 2, October 2011

for effectiveness, but also profitability. The evaluation takes the form of a stage-gate process that looks like this:

- Gate 1: initial screening
  - Stage 1: preliminary assessment
- Gate 2: second screen
  - Stage 2: business case preparation
- Gate 3: decision on business case
  - Stage 3: development
- Gate 4: post-development review
  - Stage 4: testing and validation
- Gate 5: pre-commercialization business analysis
  - Stage 5: full production and market launch
- Post-implementation review

At any of these stages, a drug candidate may be abandoned.

REGULATORY CONSTRAINTS

The second reason drug development takes too long and costs too much is regulatory. Drugs are becoming increasingly specific. On the one hand, this is a good thing; drugs target specific conditions more carefully and closely. In oncology, this means drugs that are specific to tumor types, for example.

On the other hand, this makes it harder to conduct clinical trials. As the target use for a drug is defined more finely, the candidate population of potential beneficiaries shrinks. As the numbers above describe, clinical trials must involve dozens, then hundreds, then thousands of patients to be statistically significant and acceptable to regulators.

These tests are necessary, yet patients are becoming harder to find—indeed, this is the biggest problem in clinical trials: 48 percent of sites either under-enroll the number of volunteers they seek or fail to enroll enough to complete a trial.[6] Recruitment can be so difficult that different treatment centers may end up competing against each other. At the very time that medicine is becoming more and more personalized, the specificity of new drugs means acceptable clinical testing is more difficult to accomplish.

A LIMITING BUSINESS MODEL

The third component slowing drug discovery is the underlying business model. The Big Pharma, ivory tower model involves the brute-force approach to drug development: pump out thousands of candidate drug molecules, drive through the process as described above, and hope to

---

6   "Enhancements to CenterWatch's Clinical Trials Listing Service to Improve Trial Visibility to Aid Patient Recruitment," CenterWatch, November 19, 2014, https://www.centerwatch.com/press/pr-2014-11-19.aspx.

come out with a blockbuster that will earn over $1 billion annually.

On average, the development of a single drug through conventional pathways takes more than nine years and is prohibitively expensive. Between 1997 and 2011, twelve of the biggest pharmaceutical companies in the world spent an average of $5.7 billion per drug to develop 140 new drugs.[7] No wonder pharma companies seek drugs with huge markets and large profit potential. The die is cast—Big Pharmas can't afford to pursue drugs with smaller target populations or less headroom for profit. A drug that "only" earns $100 million per year isn't worth pursuing, regardless of how much human suffering it would salve. Their sunk costs in this development model are too high.

This is why you see so much focus on developing drugs for cancer treatment and cognitive diseases. The US comprises half the world's drug market, and the FDA allows drug companies to price their drugs as they see fit. Cancer, sadly, is where the money is. Each year, 439 new cancer cases per 100,000 population are diagnosed in the United States. Cancer treatment tends not to be a cure—it's a treatment, often mostly palliative. Five-year survival rates—that is, the percentage of patients still

---

7   Nidal Al-Huniti, "Quantitative Decision-Making in Drug Development," AstraZeneca, June 20, 2013, 23.

alive five years after a diagnosis—are low. For example, five-year survival of pancreatic cancer is only 3 to 8 percent, according to various studies. In 2017, the spending on cancer was $147.3 billion, and this is only going to increase.[8] Cancer prevalence will increase as the United States population ages and as environmental factors lead to more mutations.

In other words, there's a lot of headroom for making a profit in cancer drugs. The story is similar in terms of neurodegenerative diseases such as Alzheimer's: rising incidence, no real cure, lots of profit potential. In 2015, fully 25 percent of all new late-stage drugs in the drug development pipeline were oncology drugs. Another 15 percent targeted neurodegenerative diseases. That's good for people suffering from those diseases. But what about the other 350 million patients worldwide suffering from a rare disease?

AN INFORMATION OLIGOPOLY

Many traditional publishing companies complain they can't make money anymore, thanks to the disruption of the internet. That is not the case in for those firms operating in the data analysis and scientific journal businesses. The scientific journals have a lock on the dissemination of

---

8   "Cancer Statistics," National Cancer Institute, last modified April 27, 2018, https://www.cancer.gov/about-cancer/understanding/statistics.

knowledge right now. If a researcher wants to publish in a journal, he has to pay for the privilege. If other researchers want to read the journals, they have to pay. And the journal holds the copyright to the paper itself. The rest of the publishing industry has been crying the blues, losing money, and going out of business. Not the life sciences journals. Their business model is highly profitable. But it doesn't speed up drug discovery. If anything, it hinders it.

Under the present model, the copyright belongs to the publisher, not the researcher. If I were to ask an author for a copy of a paper he published in a journal today, he could not send it to me. He doesn't own it. He pays to have it peer-reviewed and pays to get published, and others pay to read. How can this system be described as helping in drug discovery? Rather than disseminating information, scientific journals are controlling it. The process is not democratic and it is not open.

Today, these legacy structures are starting to crack. The Big Pharma monopoly on data, research, and development is about to be broken. Looking at the evolving landscape of personalized medicine and how AI and blockchain bring new developmental tools to the challenge of drug discovery, an observer can discern that different ways to bring effective drugs to market will evolve.

A NEW DRUG-DISCOVERY PARADIGM

To change the paradigm of drug discovery, we must do three things, which I detail in the following chapters.

The first is to stop looking in the rearview mirror of the drug-discovery vehicle. Let's try looking out the data windshield so we can see actual use cases and what is happening in life sciences in real time, rather than in the past. We do that by creating an automated process to extract real-time data from the entire life sciences data universe, including publications, congresses, patents, grant applications, competitive intelligence information, forums, blogs, guidelines, and so on. We crawl through all the silos, all the places where researchers, patients, hospitals, clinics, biotech firms, academics, and others gather research and patient data—and we bring it together in a single platform that structures that data in real time and is fully automated. At first glance, this task may seem impossible, but it's not. I'll come back to it later.

Second, we address the problem of information asymmetry. Rather than a few big players having a relative monopoly on information and a few companies making a lot of money by charging for the manual curation and annotation of information, we democratize data.

This may sound like an impossible task that would require thousands of analysts. It is—if you think in terms of analysts. It is not if you think in terms of artificial intelligence. Instead of using what is effectively an army of human scribes, we create an automated system to curate data from different sources, annotate and aggregate, and provide context and a frame of reference, which together creates the ability to look through the windshield and perceive new insights. An automated system breaks apart the prohibitive cost structure that has kept smaller hospitals, research centers, and the like from accessing data insights.

Here's an analogy: imagine that the only way to acquire an automobile is to have a team of specialists handcraft one for you. A car would be an incredibly rare and expensive luxury. That's the present situation for gaining access to contextualized search data. It is compiled and contextualized by hand, by "craftsmen" PhDs with specialized skills. The system I'm describing is essentially the Toyota Camry production line: mostly robots producing widely affordable cars. Almost anyone could afford to drive. Driving, and data insights, become democratized.

Third, we solve the problem of data privacy. Right now, the majority of data is proprietary information—potentially valuable, often representing extensive investment. As I've described, pharmaceutical researchers don't share data before they publish in established journals, for fear of having their ideas stolen, and nobody publishes anything about experiments that don't prove a hypothesis. If the data is an individual's—for example, a patient's medical records—multiple laws hinder the sharing of that data. In Europe, the General Data Protection Regulation (GDPR) directive went into effect in May of 2018, sharply restricting data sharing. In the United States, the Health Insurance Portability and Accountability Act (HIPPA) largely prevents the sharing of patient data. German laws are even stricter. Hospitals are limited by law in terms of how long they may save patient data, and eventually they must delete it.

The practical effect is that there is limited training data available for artificially intelligent systems to learn from. As I alluded to above, and will describe in more detail in chapter 2, AI systems get smarter by learning from data. The bigger the data training sets, the better they learn. That's why a program that reads CT scans will be more accurate if it can see the annotated diagnoses from five radiologists, rather than just the work of one radiologist.

Imagine what we could learn if we had the ability to do longitudinal analysis on a disease—if we had *all* the disease data for *all* the patients in the world suffering from a particular condition, everything about their cases, going back years and years. Imagine how much we could learn from that.

We don't have that now. But we can, through the use of blockchain technology—which I will discuss in chapter 4.

When these changes are in place—and they are already falling into place—the ecosystem of drug discovery changes fundamentally. A quick search of the news shows that the pharmaceutical business is being upended from a lot of directions. Amazon got into the pharmacy business in June 2018 with the $1 billion purchase of PillPack.[9] Google's parent company, Alphabet, has a health and life sciences research wing called Verily and is investing in the next-gen health insurance company Oscar Health.[10] Apple is using its Health app and Apple Watch to get involved in clinical trials.[11] These companies are not rebuilding the drug-discovery pipeline in the way I am describing in this book. They are, however, indicators that change—massive change—is coming.

Drug discovery and development will soon be disrupted and transformed by the release of a truly open

---

9   Claire Ballentine and Katie Thomas, "Amazon to Buy Online Pharmacy PillPack, Jumping Into the Drug Business," *New York Times*, June 28, 2018, https://www.nytimes.com/2018/06/28/business/dealbook/amazon-buying-pillpack-as-it-moves-into-pharmacies.html.

10   Brian Heater and Sarah Buhr, "Alphabet Invests $375 Million in Oscar Health," TechCrunch, August 14, 2018, https://techcrunch.com/2018/08/14/alphabet-invests-375-million-in-oscar-health/.

11   "The Future of Clinical Trials: How AI & Big Tech Could Make Drug Development Cheaper, Faster, & More Effective," CBInsights, August 7, 2018, https://www.cbinsights.com/research/clinical-trials-ai-tech-disruption/?utm_source=CB+Insights+Newsletter&utm_campaign=b62163763e-Top_Research_Briefs_08_10_2018&utm_medium=email&utm_term=0_9dc0513989-b62163763e-86278661#apple.

and innovative drug-discovery system. This will benefit pharmaceutical companies, reducing costs and speeding delivery, and thus benefiting patients by making drugs more available and affordable. When such an ecosystem matures, the chances of finding treatments and cures for everyone—not just those with the privilege of living in the developed world or knowing the right people or suffering from profitable diseases—will be within reach. The effects of this disruption will be especially significant for patients suffering from rare diseases. The effectiveness of the new ecosystem in generating new drugs will depend on two distinct and rapidly evolving technologies working in tandem: blockchain and artificial intelligence.

CHAPTER 2

THE THREE WAVES OF ARTIFICIAL INTELLIGENCE

PEOPLE WHO DON'T UNDERSTAND ANYTHING about AI tend to have a knee-jerk fear reaction to it. At some level, they are afraid that robots are going to take over the world and make slaves of all the humans. Or, perhaps more pragmatically, that the machines will take over their jobs and render them obsolete.

AI has a long way to go before we get to a *Terminator* scenario, if we ever do. As for AI displacing jobs, let's pull that scenario apart and inspect the constituent elements.

COGNITION AND WORK

We can divide cognitive work into high-level and low-level work, each requiring different capabilities. Translational capabilities, for example, translate a business problem into a data science problem. To do this well, you need to understand the business problem, the business context, the data science element, and the technology element. There is lots of thinking going on there—it's high-level work.

In the lower level are tasks such as data entry, collating data, combining data, basic analysis, and data visualization. Higher-level tasks rely on lower-level tasks, looking at all of that work and providing inferences and analysis, both prescriptive and predictive.

Which of these types of work is more enjoyable and interesting for a human being? Clearly, the higher-level work. Yet, presently, 60 percent of data scientists' and analysts' time and attention goes to researching and cleaning data—low-level, clerical tasks. Why should a company expect its employees to do lower-level work if they don't have to? What is the opportunity cost of that time and attention?

This question of opportunity cost brings to mind the work Simons and Chabris did on what they termed "inattentional blindness." Their 1999 research became an internet sensation when they released a video showing a woman in a gorilla suit walking through a basketball drill. Half of the viewers in their experiment, tasked with counting the number of ball passes, missed the gorilla entirely.[1] Is something similar happening when life sciences researchers spend their time on lower-level cognitive tasks rather than higher-level cognitive tasks? Are they failing to see the gorilla in the room—or, in their case, the insight in the data?

No one really wants to do donkey work, to be a clerk. People are more fulfilled when they are able to be creative, rather than limited to repetitive tasks. The power of AI in life sciences is to automate these lower-level cognitive tasks and empower people to use their time effectively to truly create value. This is Maslow's pyramid in action, moving up toward self-actualization. We all crave the opportunity to express our innate human creativity. AI can facilitate that.

For our purposes in life sciences—and this will be true in many industries—AI is not a tool that takes away your job. AI is a tool that automates the lower-level cognitive tasks, so you have the time and capacity to create value through the higher-level cognitive tasks.

---

1   Daniel Simons, "But Did You See the Gorilla? The Problem With Inattentional Blindness," *Smithsonian Magazine*, September 2012, https://www.smithsonianmag.com/science-nature/but-did-you-see-the-gorilla-the-problem-with-inattentional-blindness 17339770/

THE THREE WAVES OF AI

The US Defense Advanced Research Projects Agency (DARPA) characterizes the development of AI in three waves. The first wave developed systems that exhibited handcrafted knowledge (think of chess-playing programs); the second wave involved systems that engage in statistical learning (voice and face recognition); and the third wave, which is still being created, develops contextual adaptation (making decisions and being able to explain them).

These systems don't supplant one another—there are robust first- and second-wave AI systems operating throughout the world today. They do, however, build on each other. Below, I'll describe the evolution and characteristics of each.

CORE COMPONENTS OF AI

To begin, it's important to understand that artificial intelligence is built from four foundational components:

Computational power. This means both the available power itself and the price of that power. Moore's Law has shown us for decades that available power continues to rise and price continues to fall. Without this, AI doesn't happen.

Data. Data must be extracted, cleaned, and used as

training data to feed learning algorithms. The availability of data is one of the biggest challenges to developing second-wave AI, and it is fundamental to it. Without training data, AI can't learn.

Algorithms. The simplest way to think of algorithms is that they are the interface between human and computer languages. They are the instructions that people use to tell computers how to perform certain tasks.

People. This means data scientists, data translators, and so on. Without people, AI doesn't do anything.

FIRST-WAVE AI

When we talk about waves of AI, we're really describing paradigms of AI. First wave and second wave are different paradigms because first wave does not involve any learning, and second wave does involve learning.

The first wave of AI is about rules and patterns. Humans find patterns based on their knowledge or observations and define rules to match the needed outcome. Machines then are tasked with finding the information that matches the defined rules or patterns.

For example, if the task is finding email IDs within a body of text, humans define the rules that "an email address is any piece of text that contains an @ and a period, with characters before, after, and in between, and without spaces." With this coded in, a machine can find email IDs.

However, if the task were to predict the weather, for example, that would be very difficult for first-wave AI; it's impossible for humans to define all the rules that you would need to consider to predict the weather with a certain confidence.

The first modern conceptualizations of AI happened in the 1950s and 1960s. Computer scientists were able to write good algorithms. But the other components for AI were not in place. Computational power was limited and expensive, and there wasn't that much training data available. The biggest changes over the intervening decades have been the explosion of cost-effective computational power and the increase in available data.

People were writing powerful algorithms in the 1950s, but they didn't have the power or data to run them. Pretty quickly, they realized that while it was nice to have a cool algorithm, it didn't do much good if a computer needed two weeks to run it.

The first wave of AI was about optimization algorithms. This means taking a known solution to real-world problems—rules—and solving them more fluidly, efficiently, and quickly. In first wave, there are decision trees that represent rules: if you see this, then that happens, and so on. That's how rules are constructed in algorithms. For instance, if I teach a machine how viscosity depends on the density of a fluid over various temperatures and pressures, the machine learns that viscosity depends on these three factors in the following ways and can then assess viscosity by itself, given a set of temperature and pressure data.

The machine calculates an outcome based on the data and the underlying relationships, or algorithms, it has been given. This application of rules is a characteristic of first-wave AI. Importantly, first wave includes no components of machine learning. First-wave machines are not capable of exhibiting learning.

DARPA considers four categories of intelligence when evaluating the strengths of AI: perceiving, learning, reasoning, and abstracting. First wave is very good at perceiving the natural world and at reasoning because you have given the AI the rules it needs to follow. For example, if I tell the machine 1 + 1 = 2, and then type in 1 + 1 and the machine tells me "2," if I ask why, it will say "because 1 + 1 = 2." It's quite weak at learning and has zero capability to abstract from one domain to another. It can classify and calculate outcomes based on the data, but it can't understand the context of what's going on.

Today we see first-wave AI at work in logistics planning and programs like TurboTax, where programmers take a complex system (like the US tax code) and convert it into rules the computer then works through. It's a very logical form of reasoning that works through a set of facts applied to a system of rules.

This first wave of AI is good at optimizing for solutions within multivariable programming. We see it applied in fluid dynamics and space programs to run computer simulations. We saw it in the first iterations of IBM's Deep Blue, the computer program that defeated the world chess champion Garry Kasparov in 1997. At that time, Deep Blue could be taught the rules of chess and study thousands of chess games—those games were the training data. It calculated the probability of outcomes, knowing the basic rules of chess and applying a lot of computational power.

First-wave programs like the 1997 version of Deep Blue are good at reasoning within a narrowly defined problem, like how to win at chess (today's iteration of Deep Blue, by the way, is much more sophisticated). There's value in this, but also profound limitations. I come from a culture (Indian) that really values proficiency at chess. Whenever my family visited relatives, my mother always urged me to play with my cousins. When I sat down at the board, it was as if the reputation of all my chess-playing forefathers was on the line. If I lost, everyone knew about it. People made, and make, a big deal about fantastic chess players, and certainly they have a lot of skill. Remember, though, that winning at chess is a skill within a very narrowly defined problem. There is always a discrete, limited number of permutations and combinations for any game. That's why an algorithm such as Deep Blue's, driven by a lot of IBM's computing horsepower, could excel at the game. It looks at the situation on the board and asks, *If I do this move, what would happen next, and next, and next?* It relies on deep computational power and a fantastic memory—attributes Deep Blue and the human brain share in common.

What I'm describing as first-wave AI is what the American economist Herbert Simon called "bounded rationality"—situations in which problems are circumscribed by limitation of the machine (or human) doing the thinking and the environment the problem exists in (in this case, the chessboard). This was where first-wave AI excelled.

SECOND-WAVE AI

The second wave extended the first wave by allowing machines to identify patterns from data themselves, rather than relying on humans to tell them the patterns. Given enough past data (called "training data"), a machine can figure out the patterns by itself and define the rules to search (this is the training process). These rules can be a combination of thousands or millions of complex pieces, volumes of data that are incomprehensible to humans. The machine learns only for a specific goal; each algorithm is usable only for that goal, and new training is needed for every kind of goal.

If a second-wave AI system were tasked with finding email IDs within a body of text, rather than telling the system what to do, programmers could provide a few thousand email IDs to the system as training data and let it identify the pattern. Then it could find IDs itself.

If a second-wave AI program were given weather data for the last forty years for five hundred cities, it would learn the patterns of how weather changes. A programmer could then provide today's weather data for a certain city, and the machine could predict tomorrow's weather.

Rise in Computing Power and Data Volumes

The transition to second-wave AI was facilitated by the paradigm-shifting power of Moore's Law and by the evolution of the cloud. The idea of the cloud traces back to the early 1960s, when users shared access to mainframe computers. The dotcom boom of the 1990s brought about improved bandwidth, broader access to personal computing devices, and high-speed networks. But two firms were critical in bringing the cloud as we know it into existence. Salesforce.com and Amazon Web Services were lead adopters in 2008 of software as a service and infrastructure as a service, respectively. These offerings, in simplest terms, allowed Salesforce and AWS to provide computing services on a subscription basis. Rather than relying on their own servers, clients could rent the computer space they needed from server farms—the cloud—and scale as they wanted to. Rackspace, Microsoft, and Google quickly joined this field, and by 2012, the cloud was a well-established fact in modern business.[2]

If algorithms made first-wave AI possible, computational power brought second-wave AI into being. When I was at university (which wasn't really that long ago), if we wanted to run a simulation on the school's supercomputer, we might have to wait three days for the result. Today, anyone with access to Amazon Web Services or Google Cloud Platform can get the same result within minutes or hours. The cloud has massively increased the availability of computational power, as has the exponential decrease in the cost of computer power. Over the last quarter century, the cost has dropped by a factor of ten every four years, on average.[3]

---

2   Ari Liberman Garcia, "The Evolution of the Cloud: The Work, Progress and Outlook of Cloud Infrastructure" (master's thesis, Massachusetts Institute of Technology, February 2015).

3   "Trends in the Cost of Computing," AI Impacts, October 3, 2015, https://aiimpacts.org/trends-in-the-cost-of-computing/.

Second-wave AI is able to perceive things and learn from given data. You feed data in; it creates its own rules. Feed it many pictures of cats, it will learn cats and define the rules to identify a cat in a new picture. But an outside observer cannot know its rules. If you were to ask the machine why it is a cat, it will not be able to reason why.

Second-wave systems are good at perceiving the outside world and at learning from particular kinds of data sets. They have very limited capability to reason and no improved capability over first-wave systems for abstracting to other data sets.

As evolutions of the IBM computer Deep Blue continued, it took on the characteristics of second-wave AI. This was demonstrated in 2016, when it defeated the Go grand master Lee Sedol. Go is a much more complex game than chess, and the computer learned its own way of playing the game, rather than relying only on the rules it was told.

Second wave is good at voice recognition—it can hear a voice and predict who is speaking. It also can learn to recognize photographs—up to a point. There is an image-reading machine at Stanford that tends to write good captions for images, but it still makes mistakes—you might show it a picture of a baby holding a toothbrush and it will write "a young boy is holding a baseball bat." Second-wave AI is statistically very reliable, but individually unreliable. That is, over time it will have a high probability of being correct, but it may make egregious errors (toothbrush = baseball bat) on individual problems.

Second-wave AI needs a lot of training data to learn the right things and arrive at the correct conclusions, and the grooming and preparation of this data still requires a high degree of human intervention. Microsoft learned this when it released the AI bot named Tay onto Twitter. Within twenty-four hours, other Twitter users—whose comments composed the training data—had taught Tay to be a racist anti-Semite, and Microsoft took the experiment down.

Without this human help, it's entirely possible that the machine will learn the *wrong* things. If you don't have a lot of training data, the probability of success, of the predictive model being right, is low, and time-consuming human supervision will be required to ensure that the model is driving the desired results. Second-wave AI relies on having the right training data.

THIRD-WAVE AI

Third-wave AI is not yet well defined; we are experiencing its evolution from second wave as I write this book. Researchers are able to specify the outcomes of third-wave AI, but the algorithms that will achieve those outcomes are not yet well defined.

Third-wave AI deals with the ability to interpret and the ability to cross-leverage algorithms. The idea is to create a variety of AI algorithms, each solving a small, generic problem, and leverage multiple algorithms together for each goal without much training, if any at all. Small and generic algorithms can be independently reused for a lot of different problems, and predictions made through multiple generic algorithms would help humans understand the mechanism behind any prediction.

For example, one algorithm for email prediction, one algorithm for person name identification, one algorithm for text layout mapping, and one for photo interpretation can be combined to predict whether a given piece of text is a Yellow Pages listing or a profile of an individual.

When it comes to forecasting weather, a third-wave AI system could have tens of models, each predicting a single aspect of weather and interacting together to come up with a holistic forecast.

Third-wave AI builds on the algorithms and computing power that led to second wave. Data is what makes third-wave AI possible. Data is not sexy—who wants to talk about that when we can discuss algorithms? Some people assume data has always been available to train AI, but that's not true. The significance of data is not simply that there's more of it, but that the machine can do things with it that it could not do in earlier AI paradigms, leading (for the first time) to AI-generated insights.

In the first wave of AI, the people involved were computer scientists who wrote algorithms. In the second wave, engineers who could build the processing systems took prominence. In the third wave, attention has shifted to people we now call data scientists, who know what is needed to contextualize data. We also see the rise of people called "translators," who translate business problems into data problems. This is how human involvement in AI has evolved.

Contextual Adaptation

Let's return to a problem I identified earlier, the problem of looking in the rearview mirror to figure out where we're going. This is a challenge in drug development because lack of access to real-time data hinders insights. It's also a limitation for first- and second-wave AI. If you ask a second-wave AI system to predict the future, it can only do that by extrapolating quasi-linearly from the past—from the training data you have fed it.

The American psychologist and computer scientist J.C.R. Licklider quipped, in a 1960 paper, that 85 percent of his work was getting ready to think. This is certainly true with the way humans grapple with data. First, you have to find the relevant data. Then you have to obtain it. If it's not structured, you have to structure it, which means bringing it into context. Then you have to get it into a comparable form, so that you can analyze it. Only then can you begin to think.

This brings us to third-wave AI, which encompasses contextual adaptation. A second-wave system could, if properly trained, tell us with 99 percent accuracy whether an image showed a cat. But it could say nothing about why it is a cat. A third-wave AI system, when the technology is fully developed, will be able to do so. It will be able to show *reasoning*. Over time, third-wave AI will build underlying explanatory models that allow it to characterize what it is seeing and explain why. Third wave can show why it makes decisions.

In terms of artificial intelligence, third-wave AI will perceive the world well and learn from it, and reason based on what it has learned from the model it has developed; and it may be able to abstract from that model to other situations.[4] In this regard, it will be able to behave analogously to a human who, for example, learns how to play badminton and then takes that knowledge and applies it to the game of tennis.

---

4   For this section, I am deeply indebted to the explanations of AI offered by the US Defense Advanced Research Projects Agency's "A DARPA Perspective on Artificial Intelligence," https://www.youtube.com/watch?v=-Oo1G3tSYpU.

AI AND LEARNING

Within the context of AI, we use the terms "machine learning" and "deep learning." Machine learning includes the mathematical models inherent in second-wave AI, in which the machine leverages a user-provided set of parameters to identify patterns from given data. Here, a programmer or an expert defines which parameters to look at and the machine fits the data as per the mathematical framework.

There is no learning in first-wave AI, but there is in second wave. Sticking with the example of hunting for email addresses, a first-wave AI would have to be told, "look for the @ sign, with text on either side, and a period, and no spaces." A second-wave system can be told, "look at special characters (space, dots, @, !, %, etc.), numbers, and alphabets in the given data to find common behaviors."

In the case of using second-wave AI for weather prediction, the user suggests temperature, rainfall, humidity, and cloud coverage as a few of the parameters for second-wave AI to identify combinations that predict next day's weather.

Deep learning, still part of second-wave AI, is an extended version of machine learning. In deep learning, the machine itself identifies both the parameters to look at *and* what their values, combinations, or weighting should be, all from training data. Accomplishing this, however, requires much more data and much more care to ensure the machine doesn't stray from the goal.

For example, given thousands of email IDs, the machine identifies that @ should have 100 percent weighting; the absence of spaces should have 100 percent weighting; the presence of other alphanumeric characters before and after @ have a certain weight, and so on.

If asked to forecast the weather, the machine would learn that clouds today at some distance indicate higher chances of rain tomorrow, that humidity is higher the day after rainfall and decreases each subsequent day, and so on.

THE BOUNDS OF COGNITIVE PARSIMONY

Central to understanding the power of third-wave AI in drug discovery is the concept of *cognitive parsimony*—the idea that your cognition is bounded by what you know. Humans experience this all the time. We can't imagine what lies outside our universe because our knowledge is limited to our universe. A computer working with the rules that data scientists have given it can't "imagine" a different outcome than one the rules predict.

In science, cognitive parsimony is inherent to the scientific process. Imagine a research scientist beginning work. Here are the steps he undertakes:

- To begin, he'll read all the relevant literature on the subject.
- Based on what he knows from the literature, he'll look for gaps in the research.
- Based on those gaps, he'll formulate a research question.
- From the question, he'll formulate a set of hypotheses.
- From these hypotheses, he'll design an experiment.
- He conducts the experiment to prove or disprove the hypotheses, thus filling in the research gap.

The scientist is limited by cognitive parsimony. He can only read the existing research. He can only see the gaps that research reveals. The set of hypotheses he develops is similarly limited by his imagination and experience.

Now imagine a world in which the research scientist can comprehend all life sciences data, everywhere. He can see the entire data universe, visible and invisible (published and unpublished, and data trapped in silos). He can create a functionally unlimited set of hypotheses that he validates not by experimentation but by looking at the data. Reasoning expands exponentially. Cognitive parsimony is banished (assuming he has a very big brain).

This situation, unlike a game of chess, represents unbounded rationality because it embodies the ability to extract and see data in different contexts. The Stanford philosopher Jean-Pierre Dupuy describes the corresponding idea of counterfactual rationality, which can be encompassed by third-wave AI. Our human, rational way of thinking is inductive or deductive: A leads to B, B leads to C leads to D. What if A leads to F? You wouldn't imagine that in a deductive system. To test if that were plausible, you would need the capacity to analyze a massive data universe.

CAN WE TRANSCEND HISTORY?

Up to this point in our history, what we know is contingent upon our thinking within a system of bounded rationality. That is—and this is true for every human being—what you know depends, first, on the data you have in front of you and your field view—your cognitive parsimony. It depends, second, on how much you can process, either with your brain or with a computer's computational power. It depends, third, on what set of hypotheses you can form from the first two limitations: what you can see and what you can process.

If what you see and what you can process are limited by cognitive parsimony (and they are), then your hypotheses likewise will be limited. And yet, humans are not entirely limited this way. In his book *Thinking, Fast and Slow*, Daniel Kahneman describes two systems of thinking contained within human intelligence, "system one" and "system two." System one is rational. It operates within bounded rationality. You look at data and apply your decision tree, based on your experiences and knowledge of the world, to make sense of things. This is functionally akin to the "second-wave AI" version of human intelligence.

System two is the intuitive system. We all have deep knowledge inside of us, in our subconscious, which sees and makes connections and conclusions we can't necessarily explain. If we have a big decision to make in our lives, we always rely on system two. It is truly reasoning, even if it does so in ways we cannot understand. It is the "third-wave AI" version of human intelligence.

In simple terms, third-wave AI will combine the attributes of the human "system one" and "system two." It will be able to explore vast quantities of data to understand hidden relationships and to explain the logic behind those relationships. This will allow third-wave AI to create, or help create, previously unconsidered hypotheses in drug discovery. It will be able to ask questions no one has had the capability to ask, or even thought to ask.

That will be a very, very powerful tool.

This is how we make the world a better place. This is the promise of AI: unlimited data, unlimited ability to talk about this data in a context the way humans cannot, and the capacity to create hypotheses and validate them in real time.

THE PROMISE OF THIRD-WAVE AI

The application of third-wave AI is more than a promise—it's essential for progress.

DATA VOLUMES EXPLODING

First, because the volume of data in life sciences is exploding. If we don't develop a system like the one I've described, we'll be overwhelmed. The velocity at which everyone is publishing is spectacular, and it's accelerating. My math teacher used to say, "If you assume something, you make an ass of you and me," but in life sciences the effect is even worse. You have to make assumptions to proceed with your work, but then the world changes. A new study comes out; a new class of inhibitors is discovered. Or a competitor to your drug candidate suddenly gets fast-track approval, and your candidate ends up in the doldrums.

NECESSARY CONTEXTUALIZATION

Second, we need the ability to process an increasingly

deep, dense, diverse data universe in real time. But "process" means more than collecting. It means understanding, which requires contextualization.

Third-wave AI has the ability not only to escape the limits of bounded rationality, but also to see and perceive the data in a contextual model that it has learned on its own, enhances the model, perceives the data, and applies it to the model.

It learns by doing this.

What do I mean by contextualization?

Life science does not speak English, or German, or French, or Spanish. Life science speaks a language of its own; medicine has its own language. A drug could have twenty synonyms and multiple homonyms. A protein could have various isomers. You could have different targets called different names. Even a biological concept such as the way we measure kidney function, eGFR, could be describing a protein or a gene; in a different context it could be a target or a biomarker. Without some frame of reference and a shared context, the data doesn't make as much sense as it could.

Unless you contextualize the data you collect, how will you make sense of it? As I'll describe below, AI can do this—it can develop a common language for describing data and locate it within what we call "the research graph." Language offers a good analogy here. When you hear a new word, you try to figure out how it fits into your language. Is it a noun or a verb? What does it sound similar to? What does it relate to? How is it used in a sentence? You will locate that word within your understanding of language, and if you misunderstand the word and try to use it, you'll be corrected and able to relocate it properly.

You can also think of a research graph as a kind of culture. If I say the word "Christmas," that likely conjures a variety of images for you: snowy nights, choirs singing carols, the story of Jesus in the manger, Christmas cookies, decorating a tree, and so on. In life sciences, a similar process of association holds. If you tell the AI "breast cancer," it knows the genes, proteins, medicines, and so on that are associated with breast cancer—the "cultural reference," so to speak.

An AI search engine coming across a new concept will, to contextualize it, fit it into the research graph of existing knowledge that it contains. If it can't figure out what to do with a new concept, it will raise a flag, and a human can intervene to place the concept properly and help the machine learn.

Third, for life sciences to progress, we have to be able to consider diseases from multiple angles. As our understanding of the human genome has exploded, we've learned that multiple genes are susceptible to oncological mutation. At the same time, there are certain genes in the human genome and certain variations in those genes that affect the metabolism of certain drugs. All of these different things interact in the incredibly complex system that is the human body. A researcher can't just go in with a discrete set of hypotheses. You have to look the genetics, the epigenetics, the entire complex mechanism of the human body, in which all the parameters influence each other.

The complexity continues to ramify. For example, there are companies looking at tumor topology and physiology, at the genetic level and the level of protein transcription. With so many different variables and possibilities inside a complex system, you need multiple hypotheses, which can be developed from richer data.

Richer data means being able to collect more training data from different sources, contextualize it, and import it to a third-wave AI platform able to develop and validate multiple sets of hypotheses. Drug discovery today demands it. The life sciences ecosystem has become so complex we cannot understand it on our own. The effective application of AI is essential if we are to bring lifesaving drugs to market faster and more cheaply.

CHAPTER 3

AI LIMITATIONS IN DRUG DISCOVERY

THERE ARE THREE PRIMARY FACTORS THAT LIMIT AI's effectiveness at the moment in drug discovery and development: the need for an ontology for data, the problem of unpublished data and data in silos, and the challenge of data privacy.

A NECESSARY ONTOLOGY FOR DATA

A COMMON LANGUAGE

Data doesn't speak a language we would recognize. Data language is a Creole or Urdu language, a polyglot mix of other tongues. For example, in life sciences, genes speak gene ontology (an ontology is a theory about the nature and relations of beings—more about that below). Drugs have drug taxonomy. Diseases have a taxonomy called

ICD, and so on and so forth. There are different dialects and languages with which various biological concepts or entities talk among themselves, metaphorically speaking. In order to combine all of them and create a context, you need to create a language that is understood by genes, by proteins, by pathways, by diseases—a supra-Creole that brings together all of the languages and dialects spoken by life sciences entities.

A small, very intelligent child named, say, William Shakespeare, may at the age of two have approximately twenty-eight hundred concepts of a language. Over time, as he grows, he learns, so that by the time he is a young adult he has learned about half a million concepts in language (if he speaks English). Because he is Shakespeare, he has mastered the language. He can say things in new ways, combine words into new concepts that surprise and delight.

Or imagine he is a very intelligent German child named Johann Wolfgang von Goethe. By adulthood, he will have mastered 6.5 million words in his language, giving him the ability to create communication of extraordinary precision. The more experiences the child has, the more conversation he engages in, the more books he reads, the richer his language becomes and the better a speaker or writer he becomes.

Ontology works the same way, agglomerating different concepts into a single language. AI creates an ontology of the available data—a way of semantically connecting all the various taxonomies, classification schemas, and existing ontologies within the data subsets. AI uses this ontology to process millions and millions of documents and data sets, looking for relationships between diseases, treatments, conditions, chemical compounds, and so on. AI can use the ontology to understand the different data sets and look for the depths, context, and nature of relationships.

The necessary result for AI to truly work within life sciences is a meta-ontology that covers all the classification schemas, taxonomies, and ontologies that govern life science data. Without this, you cannot contextualize data.

HUMAN DATA TRANSLATORS

Lacking a common language, we seek translators. Today, translators are humans—manual curators, in the form of thousands of analysts who are medical doctors or hold PhDs in microbiology or virology or chemistry or similar fields, and who can translate the data from these different life sciences languages into one context. They are employed by firms that charge a great deal of money for their services.

These services have their limitations. They are expensive, and they require armies of translators. As the amount of available data expands exponentially, the number of translators can, at best, grow linearly. This is not a sustainable situation. A service might hire a thousand PhDs, but soon it will need two thousand as the volume of data expands, then four thousand. At the same time, the context and degree of specificity are expanding. Twenty years ago, breast cancer was considered a single disease. Now it's a set of twenty diseases. This means analysts must become more specialized to make sense of data.

If a data analysis firm doesn't hire more specialized annotators, the annotation and contextualization quality drops. If they do hire more, their costs go up. This cost can be passed along to end users, but it becomes a deadweight for all the stakeholders in the life sciences ecosystem. All the players push this deadweight to each other. It costs pharma and biotech companies, so they push it to shareholders or customers. This deadweight cost limits the availability of data—it's only accessible to those who can pay for it, the opposite of democratized data. Smaller hospitals, researchers, and individual physicians cannot afford access to the data, hampering opportunities for innovation.

THE PROBLEM OF UNPUBLISHED DATA
LACK OF INCENTIVES TO SHARE

There is presently no incentive for Big Pharmas and researchers to share data from failed clinical trials and the compounds they tested or from other relevant work, like defining the structure of a newly discovered molecule (work that is often repeated by different researchers). Published data thus only represents a portion of the valuable data that exists; only half of clinical and preclinical studies are published, and those publications are often incomplete in terms of the results.[1] We are only able to see the tip of the iceberg of the research that is actually being conducted. How many insights are hidden from us because we can't access the rest of the data? Researchers only want to publish positive results, but there is an enormous amount to be learned from failures. There's no incentive for a researcher to publish a study that proves the null hypothesis—that is, that shows the tested hypothesis was not true.[2] If you were a researcher, wouldn't you want to know what *did not* work at least as much as you want to know what *did* work?

I know of one researcher who spent two years trying to do an experiment based on another researcher's protocol.

---

1   Nicola Jones, "Half of US Clinical Trials Go Unpublished," Nature, December 3, 2013, https://www.nature.com/news/half-of-us-clinical-trials-go-unpublished-1.14286.

2   Susan Michie, Ian Roberts, Ulrich Dirnagl, Iain Chalmers, John P.A. Ioannidis, Rustam Al-Shahi Salman, An-Wen Chan, and Paul Glasziou, "Biomedical Research: Increasing Value, Reducing Waste," *Lancet* 383 (2014): 101 & ff.

By chance, she met a colleague at a conference who had experienced the same problem and solved it by tweaking the protocol slightly. That coincidence allowed her to complete her experiment—but she had spent a fruitless two years and had found success only by chance. How much further along would she be if she had been able to learn that correction two years earlier?

Institutional barriers also prevent publication. Researchers face peer-review bias, limited available time to devote to publication, fear of plagiarism, industry dominance that makes it hard for them to find their voice, and a lack of confidence in the system.

BIG PHARMA CAN'T KEEP UP

More complex annotation creates more time lag. In industries where the order of complexity is high, such as life sciences, the need for real-time responsiveness goes up. A complex system is one where the parts move together; the order of complexity reflects the unpredictability of the system. Life sciences is a complex system. Yet within Big Pharma companies and research institutes, the order of the pace of change is slower than out in the rest of the world. The threat these companies face is that if they don't change at least as fast as the external world does, their innovation may be rendered redundant. They must be dynamic and resilient. That means they must know as soon as the state of the life sciences environment changes in order to adapt to that change.

A prestigious firm can't simply say, "We have the best scientists in the world; we'll come out with a breakthrough." It doesn't work like that. You constantly have to see outside. For example, if a competitor gets fast-track approval for a drug or if somebody buys the IP of a specific class of inhibitors, that might be relevant to the target you are chasing.

Not long ago, exactly this happened. A Big Pharma firm was working on a cancer-fighting compound they thought had real potential. They were, as is normal practice, conducting competitive intelligence research on what other firms were doing, to the degree they could. The truth is, that intelligence isn't very good. It's provided by data vendors whose analysts pull together snippets describing work that has been published—looking in the rearview mirror. These are then aggregated and summarized for management to give them a sense of the research landscape.

In this situation, it's easy to miss something that might be quite significant. The problem can be as simple as human error, or as subtle as the way important details are lost in the aggregation process. There's no visibility into the underlying data, and so no way for managers to cross-check what they are being told. In this case, the Big Pharma firm was caught napping when a competitor's similar drug got fast-track approval from the US FDA. That meant their own work was almost certainly wasted effort—millions of dollars down the drain because they had not understood what someone else was doing.

LIMITED VISIBILITY

This problem isn't limited to the external world—even inside research firms, one hand often doesn't know what the other hand is doing. Enterprise data is generally not searchable inside the enterprise itself. Because publication in prestigious journals is the most important currency in science, researchers often don't share work even with their own colleagues, for fear that someone else will publish before them. In addition, the rise of various data management tools used by companies (CRM, marketing automation, email, finance support softwares, etc.) has led to the creation of separate data silos associated with those tools. Each creates independently of the others. Without a technology to integrate their data, silos sprout naturally.

The primary reason for data silos, however, is simple: competitive advantage. Most research is conducted by commercial firms, and they have no incentive to share what they know with potential competitors. Data in the research world is the most valuable of all currencies, so all the players want to keep it to themselves. Data equals power in this environment, which creates an atmosphere in which data is not always shared appropriately or effectively to bring a drug candidate toward approval, even with collaborators. These tendencies toward data hoarding and secrecy hamper innovation and efficiency.

As data volumes and complexity expand exponentially, the imperative to "see outside"—to look outside the windshield in real time—grows even as the human-centered system of manual data contextualization is less capable of keeping up.

THE PROBLEM OF DATA PRIVACY

The final major limitation to AI penetration into drug discovery is data privacy, which I alluded to in the previous chapter.

Because medical data is so innate to an individual person, regulators are particularly strict with respect to personal data privacy and data protection. In Germany, for example, hospitals must delete patient data after a specified period of time. The data cannot leave the hospital at any time. Even if the data is anonymized, that's not foolproof. These restrictions are an enormous research impediment. Any meaningful analysis of a disease that progresses over time requires a longitudinal analysis, which is impossible in the current data environment.

There are good reasons for keeping individual data private. If someone's employer knows they have an incurable disease, that person might not have opportunities to progress in their career compared to someone who doesn't have that disease. Someone with liver cirrhosis caused by drinking too much alcohol isn't going to want an employer to know about that. If an insurance company knows you smoke, they already want to charge you higher premiums. Imagine if they knew everything you'd ever been concerned about or had inquired about with a physician.

There's no reason not to support data privacy and protection laws from an individual point of view. The problem, as I've described, is that this locking off or, at best, siloing of patient data limits the size of training data sets and therefore limits the potential power of AI systems learning from that data.

Despite an understandable desire to keep their own medical records private during normal times, research shows that people who are terminally ill are willing to share their data because they know how important it is to do so in order to help others. They understand that studies need patients and need data to find effective treatments.

Those who are not terminally ill don't share this realization. Siloing doesn't just happen with patient data—it's a big problem with research data, which is often treated as valuable intellectual property.

AI AND DIAGNOSIS

While the problems of ontology, data siloing, and privacy are the most significant obstacles to AI, there are others. One in particular is less directly associated with drug discovery and development, and more symptomatic of human hesitation to trust their health to a machine.

Imagine an AI system tasked with understanding tumors. A radiologist trains the learning system with a large volume of collected data. The radiologist tags tumors in different radiographs as benign, malignant, the specific type of tumor, and so on. The AI system studies the tags and learns from thousands of images; using its new reasoning abilities, it can then diagnose when a tumor is malignant or benign and what kind of tumor it is. If the tumor appears malignant, the attending physician will recommend the patient have a biopsy. If it appears benign, the physician likely will not recommend a biopsy. Many US hospitals already employ such supportive AI-based screening techniques.

Any agent, human, or machine that evaluates tumors generates a certain percentage of false positives—grade 1 errors—and false negatives, grade 2 errors, which are considerably worse. A false positive would say the tumor was malignant when it is really benign. The patient subsequently suffers not-insignificant downsides: stress, a biopsy, maybe even surgery—but the tumor isn't going to kill the patient. A false negative, on the other hand, concludes the tumor is benign when it is actually malignant. Imagine that a patient is told his tumor is benign, so he doesn't get a biopsy; he goes home and ignores it. In fact, his tumor is malignant, and without timely treatment, he will die. This is a much more significant downside than a false positive.

One study of breast cancer diagnosis showed that the current accuracy rate of AI machines diagnosing malignancies is 92 percent. When I describe a tumor-reading machine, many people become uneasy. After all, if the physician makes a mistake, we know whom to blame, or even whom to sue. But who is to blame if the *machine* makes a mistake?

If we're talking about a question of life and death, should we leave the judgment to a machine? Second-wave AI is statistically very reliable but individually can be unreliable. Should we leave our fate to the accuracy of an algorithm that's doing the first-level screening? Or would we rather rely on the experience of a physician?

However, bear in mind the alternative to having an AI read your report is not a perfect physician. It is an imperfect physician. Physicians alone have a 96 percent accuracy rate on diagnosing malignancy. A physician reading the radiograph could also make mistakes that lead to life-threatening false negatives. Physicians do this all the time, and because of that they often err on the side of testing, "just to be sure." If they don't err on the side of caution, the patient may get a false negative and die without timely treatment.

Look at how the doctor gains her experience. It's remarkably similar to how the AI gains experience; the doctor's mind simply takes longer to build the base of reference knowledge.

A doctor glances at a skin condition and knows immediately that it is rosacea, or listens to a child's cough and detects pertussis. The doctor has been practicing what the author Clayton Christensen calls "experiential medicine" in his book *The Innovator's Prescription*. He has been *learning by doing* for a long time. As patients, we take comfort in that length of experience. We want to be able to look in her eyes, to hear her voice, to be given confidence by her charm. The doctor has learned from a lifetime of experiences. A machine learns the same way, only faster, with better recall, and from more people. What the machine doesn't have is, quite literally, the human touch. That makes us uncomfortable with trusting the machine, even if it becomes statistically more accurate than the flesh-and-blood doctor.

Physicians misdiagnose four of every hundred tumors, and machines miss eight out of every hundred. Yet—and here is the key—working together, physicians and machines have a 99.5 percent accuracy rate.[3] Together, they misdiagnose only one out of every two hundred tumors.

---

3   Bonnie Prescott, "Better Together: Artificial Intelligence Approach Improves Accuracy in Breast Cancer Diagnosis," Harvard Medical School, June 22, 2016, https://hms.harvard.edu/news/better-together; Christopher Wanjek, "AI Boosts Cancer Screens to Nearly 100 Percent Accuracy," LiveScience, June 21, 2016, https://www.livescience.com/55145-ai-boosts-cancer-screen-accuracy.html.

The utility of medicine, generally, is not that it adds value to your life. It's that it prevents value from being taken away. Medicine that saves your life prevents you from dying. When you lose a life, the pain is infinite. If you suffer from an infirmity, the reduction in utility creates a huge reduction in your quality of life.

From the perspective of prospect theory, then, what we as patients have to lose if a diagnosis is wrong is very great, even infinitely great. This means that AI systems, as they are deployed in hospitals and clinics, must err on the side of creating more false positives and fewer false negatives. Because the potential loss of a false negative diagnosis is so large, we must bend the AI system's decision curve to avoid those. Machines can be taught selective wisdom. But the machine must be taught. It must be trained to factor in all the aspects that need to be checked. And we must learn to trust it.

THE SOLUTION OF DEMOCRATIZED DATA

What would it mean if we could eliminate these obstacles?

Consider the famous case of Steve Jobs's pancreatic cancer. This is one of the deadliest cancers in the world. So many people we know have died from it—Jobs, Patrick Swayze, Sally Ride, Alan Rickman, Wolfgang Pauli, Aretha Franklin, and thousands more. They are separated by space and time, and their treatment options are limited by constraints on the knowledge of their physicians. What if there were an engine that drew together all the data, all the therapies and treatments and options from across space and time to inform their treatment?

Imagine this is possible not only for the rich and famous facing pancreatic cancer, but for anyone. This is the moral imperative to "democratize data." Not to give data away, but to give people a more equal opportunity at finding and participating in a treatment or cure. When I speak of democracy, I think of equal opportunity. I look at what happened with the woman in Vienna, whom I described in chapter 1, and I ask, how can the patient in a rural clinic have the same insights into the treatment of her disease as the patient with the very best physicians, in the very best treatment center? How can the physician in a remote clinic have access to the same insights as an oncologist at Mount Sinai, Sloan Kettering, or MD Anderson? How can a small biotech startup access the same research as a Big Pharma?

That's what lies at the heart of democratizing data.

The paradigm of third-wave AI is that it will allow us to build context for vast troves of previously unrelated data, allowing for the opportunity to see and validate multitudes of permutations and combinations of hypotheses—and validate them in real time. AI will allow us to cross-pollinate data sets. Imagine if you could parse all the extant scientific literature to search for comorbidities in hospital settings. You'd have an idea of what had been researched and where the gaps exist, and then create a heat map of comorbidities in terms of the available evidence. You could create hypotheses and validate with patient data in real time.

At the moment, we are in the second wave of AI. To develop the third wave of AI will require huge data training sets. That, in turn, means that data that is presently siloed must be made available. The question becomes how do we tap all the different data sets in real time in a way that is not considered to be a challenge but an opportunity? Once all the data is mobilized and democratized, we will be in a position to develop the third-wave AI that will allow researchers to look forward out of the cockpit windshield.

These three limitations—the need for an ontology for data, the problem of unpublished data, and the problem of data privacy—have been substantial hurdles to the implementation of AI in drug discovery. They are not, however, insurmountable. To create incentives to share data, we must turn to another evolving technology: blockchain.

CHAPTER 4

THE ROLE OF
BLOCKCHAIN IN
OPENING UP DATA

YOU'VE ALMOST CERTAINLY HEARD OF BITCOIN, THE cryptocurrency based on blockchain technology. Blockchain technology and cryptocurrency are not the same thing, but the technology has gotten a bad reputation thanks to the fact that some cryptocurrencies have been fraudulent. At the time of this writing, there are around twenty-five hundred cryptocurrencies worldwide.[1] Bitcoin, Ripple, and Ethereum are among the better known. For many coins, the value is based on the utility of the underlying platform and the appeal of peer-to-peer validation, rather than central-agency validation. Bitcoin, for example, has no

---

1   "All Cryptocurrencies," Investing.com, https://www.investing.com/crypto/currencies.

underlying assets. Its value lies in the users' trust in the system. It is possible to design a token or coin in this realm with whatever attributes you wish. Many of them have no underlying assets, no central banks or managing agency (although others do have these attributes). People may invest in coins as speculative plays, as happened with Bitcoin, which hit a high of almost $20,000 per coin in December 2017 before dropping below $4,000 a year later.

This is all quite sexy and has attracted a lot of speculative investment that has clouded our comprehension of the true power underlying Bitcoin and the other cryptos. People have been working on business models based on creating a cryptocurrency as a get-rich-quick investment, rather than investing in the fundamentally disruptive power of the underlying blockchain technology.

BLOCKCHAIN TECHNOLOGY

Imagine two people want to play a game of chess. In order to play, they must agree on the state of the board. If I say the white queen is on E5, you have to agree, or we can't play together. In financial dealings, this necessary agreement historically has been managed by a centralized ledger. For your checking account, the bank holds the "golden ledger"—the true reflection of the state of your checkbook. Your own ledger, inside your checkbook, might say something different, but the bank's ledger is the one that rules the game. You either have to reconcile your ledger against the bank's or convince the bank that they are in error. This system is inefficient, expensive, and vulnerable.

An alternative solution to the golden ledger is a permissioned, replicated, shared, and decentralized ledger. There is no one ledger. All the participants have access to a shared ledger (that they hold individually and collectively), and all agree to a single protocol that allows them to agree on the true state of the ledger at any given moment. This system is characterized by consensus, provenance, immutability, and finality.

What I've described is, in very simple terms, the core of Blockchain technology. Blockchain was introduced to the world by "Satoshi Nakamoto," an apparent pseudonym for a creator who has never been identified and who published a paper in October 2008 on a cryptography mailing list. The paper described Bitcoin and the underlying blockchain technology, which had these critical characteristics:

- Peer-to-peer spending (that is, a currency that circumvents banks) up to that point was limited by the fact that a third party (such as a bank) was needed to, among other things, prevent double spending. This problem is eliminated in blockchain by creating an ongoing chain of time-stamped, tamper-proof "proof of work" or "proof of stake" blocks containing the transactions or (critically, for our purposes) any electronic piece of data.

- The blocks in the record realistically cannot be changed. While it's theoretically possible to do so, it would take so much computing power that it becomes prohibitively expensive and thus not worth attempting. To change the record would require at least 51 percent of all the computational power in the network involved in the chain. So while it could be done, it would be very, very hard and very, very expensive.

- The longest chain proves the sequence of events, and so long as the majority of computers on the peer-to-peer network are not part of an attack trying to change the chain, that chain is defended. A robust network outpaces all attackers. This creates trust in the ownership, the chain of ownership, and the record of how the block has been spent.[2]

The net effect is that blockchains provide an immutable register, such as a Bitcoin. In the case of a cryptocurrency, "work" can include spending all or part of the coin. But there are other more interesting applications of the technology.

---

2 Satoshi Nakamoto, "Bitcoin: A Peer-to-Peer Electronic Cash System," (2008), https://bitcoin.org/bitcoin.pdf.

BLOCKCHAIN AS A SECURE PUBLISHING TOOL

Blockchain is a shared, very secure distributed register. Blockchain has very specific usages in the context of the challenges we face in life sciences, primarily the issue related to people not wanting to share data. This is a problem blockchain easily can solve.

The first thing to understand about the value of blockchain is that it establishes the authorship of data. Using blockchain publishing, we can establish the rightful authorship of particular data that no one can contest.

As an example, let's say that using an EOS blockchain, I publish ten different documents and data sets that represent the results of a failed experiment. I don't actually publish the document on EOS blockchain, because blockchains are not meant to be repositories for documents. They are only repositories for the transactions. Think of them as distributed ledgers living on computers all over the web. To publish, I actually use two systems together, EOS blockchain and InterPlanetary File System (IPFS).

To secure the document itself, I use the IPFS, a distributed file system paralleling blockchain. I encrypt the document on IPFS using 32-bit encryption and a program installed on my browser call Tru-Agent. When I do that, the IPFS returns a very long alphanumeric string, called a hash key. This string is what I store on EOS, and that is how I establish the location of the document. I create a second hash key that is called the private key; it controls access to the document. If I want to share the document with someone, I can provide them the private key.

When I load the hash onto the EOS blockchain, I establish my identity using a security key, and the block adds a time stamp. Now there is a record of who I am, what I did, and when I did it. Once this data is uploaded onto the blockchain, the security key is so powerful that there is no existing computing power able to hack it. The record is not deletable. Nobody else can access the document unless they have a license to do so.

How does someone else comprehend what I've published, since I've protected it so well? I publish a summary. I used Tru-Agent to encrypt and upload the documents to the IPFS. Tru-Agent resides on my computer, and it extracts indexes, or metadata, of the documents I uploaded, based on the life sciences ontology. Using that ontology—that shared, Creole-type language—it builds indexes and sends them to the Innoplexus server (where we run a clearinghouse for data).

Innoplexus then uses those indexes to create a catalog of available data. If consumers of data want to search for an experiment or a concept, Innoplexus can provide relevant listings because we have all the indexes for all the uploaded metadata submitted to the blockchain, without having the actual data in hand. In addition, based on the metadata and the indexes we have received, Innoplexus uses an AI-based valuation engine to predict the dollar value of an experiment. This serves as guidance for both the authors of the data and the consumers, so that they can come to an agreement for the author to issue a license to access the data and subsequently share the private key. Whatever compensation arrangement they reach—which could involve money or cryptocurrency, or simply credit—happens separately between the parties. There's an advantage here to using cryptocurrency because it creates another record of what has happened that cannot be altered or deleted. Once an agreement is reached, the document can be made available immediately to the purchaser, and the transaction is immutably registered in the block, so that everyone knows that consumer A bought the data that belongs to author B. There is no time delay.

Wherever the data goes after that, the blockchain has established the primary author's ownership of it. At every point in time, anyone can see who the rightful owner is and has been. It cannot be stolen.

DISRUPTING PUBLISHING

Blockchain has the power to be disruptive on many fronts.

In life sciences, it eliminates the intermediary, such as the publisher or data annotation company, who rations access to data. Blockchain has shown there is no need for an intermediary if two parties want to transact. This is true with Bitcoin (no banks), and it is true with life sciences data—if I were in the life sciences publishing business, say, *The New England Journal of Medicine* or *Nature* or *The Lancet*—I would be very concerned about these developments, and with good reason.

Historically, the publisher has controlled access to data, determining who got to see what, and when. With blockchain, that is out the window. The publisher, or any intermediary who controls data, has been cut out of the equation. The data and ownership record are almost unhackable (unlike publisher and banking sites). To date, scientific journals have been disproportionately powerful because they have owned everything. With blockchain, we take power back by incentivizing scientists to share their data directly in a fully secured manner. This is new, it is disruptive, it is what healthcare wants, and it is what healthcare needs. It will result in better therapies and better drugs for patients coming to market faster and more efficiently.

This is what democratizing data looks like.

For our purposes in life sciences, blockchain technology

offers the opportunity to solve the data siloing and unpublished data problems I described in previous chapters. Imagine you are a biotech company or conduct research at a university. Here are the three big changes blockchain makes possible.

1. You'd like to understand the landscape of work that is being conducted right now. At the moment, you're limited to reading about it in scientific journals eighteen to twenty-four months after the fact. **Blockchain can help you by making unpublished metadata searchable in real time.** No longer are you looking in a time-delayed rearview mirror.

2. You'd like to know about specific experiments others are conducting right now. If you are going to invest in a certain avenue of research, it would be incredibly helpful to know if others are blazing a similar path. Are they succeeding or failing? Why? **Blockchain can create incentives to share all research, successful and failed alike.**

3. Finally, you'd like to know whom to collaborate with. If another researcher is doing work that can aid you in your work, you want to know about that. Your research will become faster and more effective. **Blockchain can create incentives for both sides to connect with each other, rather than hiding what they are doing to protect their IP.** Blockchain democratizes data.

There are other benefits too. Blockchain can create a revenue stream from research results, even from experiments that did not prove their hypotheses. It can save time and costs by allowing researchers to avoid repeating experiments that have been conducted but not published. And researchers can enhance their reputations without having to fight to be published in traditional journals.

Let that all sink in for a minute.

Blockchain technology holds the key to completely changing the terms under which drug development now happens. Researchers would have access to more data in real time (that is, they could look out the windshield); they would know what was not working, not simply what worked, saving enormous money, energy, and time on redundant or wasted effort; and they could connect the dots by seeing the entire research landscape in real time.

This sounds great, right? The reason it isn't already happening is there presently is no formal, secure, mutually beneficial way to share unpublished research and findings and other data among the life sciences community. Remember, the incentives within the drug-discovery ecosystem do not align correctly for optimum drug discovery. At the moment the public wants lifesaving cures, Big Pharmas want blockbuster drugs to recoup their massive investments, researchers and academics want to publish papers, patients want privacy—and everyone is afraid that their data will be stolen.

HOW BLOCKCHAIN CHANGES RESEARCH INCENTIVES

The system we are developing at Innoplexus relies on blockchain to create a new set of blockchain-based incentive models that encourage data sharing. Data sharing allows us to build larger pools of training data for the AI. The AI, in turn, will be able to develop and use a meta-ontology to see the entire life sciences landscape in ways humans never have been able to do, and to generate and validate new hypotheses in the search for drugs.

But I'm getting ahead of myself.

As I described above, there's presently no incentive to share metadata, which is the data describing underlying data. If a researcher has already published results, there's no incentive to share the underlying data sets with anyone else. The researcher got what he wanted, which is publication. If the researcher's experiment failed, there's no incentive to share the data about that either.

Imagine if the researcher *did* share the metadata about the failed experiment—that is, a sufficient description of it that it's useful for other analysts. Another researcher might say, "Hey, I'm working on something similar; can I see your data?" Now an opportunity exists to monetize the failed experiment.

Blockchain can create a market that didn't exist before for data that was not searchable or shareable. If you are a researcher who has conducted a failed experiment, you can publicize your metadata about the experiment using blockchain. The block establishes you as the original owner of the IP. Another researcher may approach you to buy the underlying data. Perhaps you'll just make some money. Perhaps that researcher will discover something worthy of publication after all. Because blockchain has established your IP on your data, it can't be stolen. Instead, you're going to be listed as a coauthor on the paper. Which, after all, is what you want.

Those are powerful incentives to share what previously seemed worthless or was something you were afraid would be stolen.

The possibilities get even more interesting, though, when we realize that the data might be useful for a third researcher who is working on something entirely different.

Remember how the rationally bounded scientific process classically works: the researcher reviews existing literature and looks for holes in the body of knowledge, derives a research question, formulates hypotheses for that question, plans experiments to validate the hypotheses, conducts the experiment to collect data, and uses the data to prove or disprove the hypotheses.

However, that data does not have to be bound uniquely to those hypotheses. The same data can be used to test a completely different set of hypotheses if combined with another set of data—if it's visible for use. Consider the case of Viagra, which was originally developed by Pfizer to treat hypertension, but then found to have positive effects on erectile dysfunction. In that case, the unexpected effects were obvious and the drug was (very) profitably repurposed. In most cases, they won't be obvious, so access to data will be essential to test alternative hypotheses.

The story of science is often told as a story of serendipity, flashes of insight, moments of brilliance. Why shouldn't we try to create the conditions conducive to such insight? The invention of functional magnetic resonance imaging (fMRI) is an example of this. Medical doctors who knew something about how the brain works knew that blood flows to active zones. If a specific area in the brain is active—let's say the motor cortex when you voluntarily move—neurons start to transmit a lot of signals. This requires a lot of ATP (adenosine triphosphate). ATP is obtained from glucose using a lot of oxygen. The more neuronal activity, the more oxygen is required. What delivers the oxygen? Blood, because the brain doesn't store glucose or oxygen. When the motor cortex is very active, the blood flow into that area will increase. Bringing a lot of oxygen requires oxyhaemoglobin as a transporter. That's what physicians know.

Now comes a physicist saying, "I know that oxyhaemoglobin is diamagnetic and has no magnetic momentum, whereas deoxyhaemoglobin is paramagnetic, transports no oxygen, and has a significant magnetic momentum." Couple this knowledge with MRI technology and one can visualize the areas in the brain that are active. A physician alone would never have come up with such an idea; for that, physicists were necessary. Physicists knew that blood carrying a lot of oxygen had a different magnetic moment. They combined these insights to imagine how to create real-time images of blood flow.

Rather than hope for such positive collisions, we should create the conditions for those conditions by making data more broadly visible. If researchers from across domains can access data more broadly, insights are more likely to happen. When AI can access that data, entirely new hypotheses will be revealed.

PATIENT INCENTIVES

If a patient is participating in a lung cancer trial today, she does not have an incentive to tell the truth about her habits. If she smokes cigarettes, does she really want the researchers to know that? Probably not, if she's afraid that her insurer will find out, because then her premiums will shoot up.

Now imagine this situation within a blockchain-supported ecosystem. We create a smart contract that incentivizes the patient: if the trial goes well and the drug goes to market, the patient can earn a share of the revenues (through participation rights in the form of tokens) from the sale of the drug. Now the patient is not just a guinea pig; he has a stake in getting it right. She has real incentive to give honest input because everyone knows that if she isn't honest, even if the drug is approved, it won't stay long in the market if it is ineffectual or has unacceptable side effects.

Presently, it's hard to find patients to participate in research trials, especially for more obscure diseases. Now, patients, who were once guinea pigs at best, have real financial incentive to volunteer for trials, in addition to the incentive of helping bring a drug to market that could help them.

As part of the contract, the researcher keeps the patient's

data in a secure, blockchain-protected way. The full control of whether to correct, delete, transfer, or share that data lies with the patient.

BLOCKCHAIN AND AI TOGETHER

Blockchain, with its potential to change incentives and create new markets for data, is a robust solution to the problem of limited data availability. It's also deeply disruptive to the medical publishing industry, and I don't expect them to like it. They make a lot of money doing what they do. But I believe their business model hinders, rather than helps, drug discovery.

Journals provide value when they vet work for publication, but is this really the only valid model for disseminating knowledge? (Sometimes their vetting is less than effective, and sometimes they don't look as hard as they should at the underlying data. The scandal around the Italian surgeon Paolo Macchiarini, who fraudulently published work for years, claiming he was using stem cells to rebuild patients' windpipes, drew into question the integrity of *The Lancet* and other journals where he had made his claims.)[3]

---

3   John Rasko and Carl Power, "Dr Con Man: The Rise and Fall of a Celebrity Scientist Who Fooled Almost Everyone," *Guardian*, September 1, 2017, https://www.theguardian.com/science/2017/sep/01/paolo-macchiarini-scientist-surgeon-rise-and-fall.

The blockchain-enabled system we're proposing creates an entirely new channel for sharing data—and more of it, and faster—in the hunt for drugs. Blockchain and artificial intelligence together can create the conditions for a new drug-discovery and development ecosystem.

CHAPTER 5

//////////////

BLOCKCHAIN PLUS AI IN DRUG DISCOVERY

THOSE THREE DEVELOPMENTS I DISCUSSED IN THE previous chapter—publishing data in real time, creating incentives to share, and democratizing data—solve problems that drug researchers see in front of them. When blockchain is combined with AI, together they enable the development of entirely new ways to seek lifesaving drugs. This is the transformative power of blockchain plus AI.

When blockchain is applied to open up life science data silos, the effects will be powerful:

- Drug development will be faster and more efficient,

because redundant efforts will be visible and can be eliminated.

· The variability of ideas going into the innovation funnel will increase, thus increasing the likelihood of successful drug discovery. This variability is a function of democratizing data, insofar as everyone in life sciences now has the opportunity to understand the full landscape, to see what others are doing, and to make connections and target contributions.

The increase in available data is crucially important, laying the groundwork for the successful application of AI to drug discovery. In the simplest terms, blockchain opens up enormous treasure troves of data; AI then figures out how to read, understand, and seek relationships within that data.

As I described in chapter 4, blockchain mobilizes data, including unpublished data. AI can be leveraged to structure that data (via extraction, crawling, computer vision, and so on) and can put it into the frame of reference we call the research graph using the life sciences ontology I described in chapter 3. A good analogy is a jigsaw puzzle. Previously, only some of the pieces of the puzzle were visible. Blockchain brings more pieces of the puzzle to the table, and second-wave AI helps figure out where within the picture they belong. The net effect is a bigger picture with more insights and relationships. Second-wave AI will be able to analyze connections between a drug and a disease that previously had been hidden because nobody had all the data points to come up with that connection—for example, a drug that is effective in oncology may also be effective for treating Alzheimer's disease.

Eventually, third-wave AI will be able to look at the data, develop its own hypotheses, and validate those hypotheses against that data.

The life sciences ontology semantically connects all the various taxonomies, classification schemas, and existing ontologies within data sets. Let's say there's a relationship between a drug and a particular disease or a particular gene. The AI can extract whether the relationship is strong or weak by, for example, looking at the frequency of the terms coinciding in publications. Critically—and this is the exponential power of the application of AI—it can look for relationships where researchers have not previously thought to look.

Imagine you now have all the scientific publications ever published over time, plus all the unpublished data of researchers. You have patient data, everything that's happening in clinical trials or presented in scientific congresses—the entire published and unpublished life sciences universe. If you want to research comorbidities of various diseases, you parse this data with AI to find which diseases co-occur. You can do a Bayesian analysis to look at clusters, or heat maps of associations, or a weak-signal analysis or an outlier analysis. You can seek evidence that is counterfactual. From all of this, you can form hypotheses you then test with patient data.

All of this can be done with AI in real time. None of this can be done by humans alone.

LOOKING OUT THE WINDSHIELD AT LAST

With blockchain and AI working in concert, drug development becomes forward-looking—that is, it gazes out the windshield—in three senses.

First, no more blind spot. There is no time lag between when research is done and when others in the field potentially could gain access to it. When I wrote my PhD, I spent six months just understanding the existing research in publication, and by the time I finished reading, five more relevant papers had come out. In life sciences, this problem is much worse. By one estimate, a new research paper is published every thirty seconds.[1] It's impossible for a human to monitor and understand everything that is going on, let alone putting all of this data into relationships and uncovering novel insights.

---

1   "Data to Drugs," BenevolentAI, https://benevolent.ai/.

Second, we can see all the data and the relationships within them. When you drive a car fast, your field of view becomes narrower; using blockchain and AI, we can drive fast and still have a wide field of view. We can employ the power of AI to understand everything that is happening in life sciences at once.

Third, all the actors in drug development have an equal opportunity to contribute because the data has been democratized, and all of them now have incentives that are aligned with the public good, rather than to their parochial interests. There is consistent focus on getting efficacious, cost-effective drugs onto the market faster.

Everything in drug discovery changes fundamentally.

PROOF OF CONCEPT: CANCERCOIN

What I am describing is more than a pipe dream. In 2018, I helped created a Swiss corporation, CancerCoin, which is a pilot project of our larger vision at Innoplexus. This spinoff is the world's first virtual pharmaceutical company.

Its first task will be to fight pancreatic cancer. As I noted in the introduction, there has been almost no advancement in pancreatic cancer treatment for decades—since at least

1971.[2] We decided to start here because if we are going to prove out this concept, we intend to set an example when we do. Pancreatic cancer is likely to soon be the second-highest cause of cancer-related mortality, after lung cancer, in the United States. It is especially deadly, with a five-year survival rate in the low single digits. The disease often is not detected until advanced stages, lowering survival rates even further. In some countries, as few as 30 percent of patients have access to therapies, and only 4.5 percent of patients with the disease enroll in clinical studies that could help them and others. We are going to take on the toughest opponent, not the easiest.

To begin, the top study groups and key opinion leaders (KOLs) in the world presently working on pancreatic cancer have access to the CancerCoin cockpit. Within that cockpit, they'll be able to see dashboards built from all the published and unpublished data on the subject. The dashboards are based on a blockchain- and AI-enabled platform that combines the whole published and unpublished universe in one place. It enables the users to have this universe annotated and ready for analysis, at their fingertips. And that's what we do, by building continuous analytics applications on top of that data ocean to gain insights. For example, who the KOLs are for a specific

2   "Cancer Survival for Common Cancers," Cancer Research UK, last modified April 29, 2014, https://www.cancerresearchuk.org/health-professional/cancer-statistics/survival/common-cancers-compared#heading-Three.

type of tumor; who drives the sentiment in the scientific world regarding specific drugs, methods, or technologies; which drugs have potential to be repurposed; and so on.

All of the CancerCoin participants share their data, and all of them work in a coordinated fashion. None of the groups replicates each other's work unnecessarily, and all of them benefit from knowing what the others are doing, efficiently dividing labor and assets.

In addition, we are aligning incentives. The study groups receive tokens that provide them with incentives to share data and promise an upside if a drug results from the work. In the old model of drug discovery, a research center is paid to work on a piece of drug development—they may be given €1 million to conduct an in vivo preclinical trial, and that is the end of their engagement. At CancerCoin, they get the €1 million, and they'll also benefit from the drug's success down the line.

Charity is well and good, but unless we incentivize all the stakeholders in an ecosystem, their hearts will not beat to get a drug out fast for patients.

What we are doing is, at the time of this writing, unique. There are other efforts in this direction, but nothing quite like CancerCoin, and none using the life sciences ontology approach.

This is the beginning of creating a virtual AI- and blockchain-based pharmaceutical company. Of course, there are skeptics—traditionalists who don't understand blockchain or AI, who think these are buzzwords and that the old systems of drug discovery will deliver the results we want. We also face opposition from the data analytics teams inside existing pharmaceutical companies. Our message to them is that blockchain and AI are coming, but not to replace them. As I discussed earlier in the book, these technologies will free life sciences researchers from some of their lower-level cognitive work, creating opportunities for them to spend more time on higher-level cognitive work, which will improve the pace and prospects of drug discovery and development.

CONCLUSION

YOU ARE IN THE COCKPIT OF AN AIRCRAFT, PILOTing it over the earth. Looking out the windshield, you can see the landscape unfolding in real time: rivers and forests below, stars and planets above, mountains and ocean in the distance. Your dashboard is filled with analytical instruments that feed you data: speed and altitude, direction, the outside temperature, rate of climb or descent, pitch and yaw, engine speed, fuel burn rate, radar images, weather forecasts.

You, as the pilot, do not need to guess what the weather is going to do. You do not need to dead-reckon your course. You do not need to calculate whether you have enough fuel to reach your destination. The machine does all this for you. You are free to digest all of the information at hand to chart your course. You analyze all you see to decide where you want to go and how you want to get there.

I began this book with the image of a researcher driving a car by watching the rearview mirror. I want to do more than show the scientist the road ahead; I want the scientist to get out of the car and into the cockpit of an aircraft. The cockpit is a platform for sharing, seeing, and understanding all life sciences data in real time. This is my vision for science: high-speed, highly efficient, everything working together in the quest for answers, with the scientist at the center of the system doing the highest-level thinking.

The existing system of drug discovery is failing us. The incentives of various actors are misaligned: researchers want publications, test centers compete for patients, patients demand privacy, and drug manufacturers can only seek the highest-profit drugs because of the massive costs inherent in development.

Change is coming. My vision uses AI to automate low-level cognitive tasks to free researchers up to do critical thinking. It uses blockchain to democratize data, opening the floodgates of information to jump-start innovation and widen the innovation funnel. It creates new incentives that align all the actors in the same direction. It allows real-time understanding of the entire research ecosystem. And it employs third-wave AI to develop entirely new hypotheses that can lead to breakthroughs.

CancerCoin is the beginning of a movement. It is the first

attempt to implement the philosophy I have described in this book.

- First, we create the cockpit—a platform on which all researchers can see and share data.
- Second, researches work in a coordinated fashion with aligned incentives to make their drug discoveries successful.
- Third, we acquire assets from "failed" drug candidates that look promising or useful (for instance, a treatment that was unsuccessful for most patients but helpful for a smaller subgroup of patients) and share that information in the cockpit. It may be that such a drug can be repurposed for a specific subgroup and brought to market.
- Fourth, the top study groups on pancreatic cancer (to begin with) share the data, working in a coordinated way to be faster and more efficient than anyone else in bringing drugs to market.

Our goal is to make real progress in ending human suffering.

THE MORAL CASE FOR AI PLUS BLOCKCHAIN IN DRUG DISCOVERY

Change is unsettling, even frightening. Humans often express an innate tendency to resist it. The changes we are bringing to the drug-discovery business will, when they are broadly implemented, radically reshape a multibillion-dollar global industry.

Is what I am proposing too disruptive? No. Now is the time to disrupt. Now more than ever.

I started this journey because a very close friend faced a very deadly disease. One of the things I learned along the way was that when people are healthy, only a negligible proportion of healthy people is willing to share their data with researchers. When people are on their deathbeds, a much higher proportion is willing to share the same data. Those who are dying understand the collective benefit such sharing provides—if not for them, then so no one else will have to suffer as they are suffering.

When you or someone close to you is deathly ill, the problem I describe in this book becomes all too real. We need lifesaving drugs. We need them faster. We need them cheaper. We need more of them. When you are facing the Grim Reaper, those truths are more important to you than almost anything.

Humans have short perspectives. If you find AI or blockchain intimidating or frightening, think about someone you know who died from cancer. Think about how you are going to feel when disease and death come to your door. Think about what we can build now to ward it off. That is the right thing to do.

ACKNOWLEDGMENTS

THIS BOOK IS A SYNOPSIS OF HOW ARTIFICIAL intelligence and blockchain can transform drug discovery and development. It is a synopsis of eight years of experimentation and tinkering with my friend and co-founder of Innoplexus, Gaurav Tripathi, whom I first met on my first day of undergraduate studies at Indian Institute of Technology, Bombay. We tried different approaches and failed in most of them miserably. Often we had self-doubts, but the deep desire to create an impact kept us going. This book, as well as Innoplexus, would never have happened without Gaurav.

Similarly, this book would not have been possible without a number of colleagues at Innoplexus who have contributed in significant ways in this journey: Dr. Tapashi Mandal, Dr. Rupesh Tyagi, Anjori Pasricha, Anshit Garg, Mohit Jhunjhunwala, Elfin Garg, Varsha Rohani, Nupoora

Udas, Vatsal Agarwal, Dr. Om Sharma, Abhijit Keskar, Dr. Juergen Raths, Lawrence Ganti, Ashwin Rathod, Silke Otte, Holger Hoffmann, Timon Schicht, Nitish Jain, Jackie Jordan, Shannon Larusso, Anne Licata, and Giselle Canahuati, to name a few. Colleagues such as Timon remind me of the selfless drive to create an impact. A very special thanks to the entire Innoplexus team spread over three continents for helping us bring to life this wonderful platform that will make a positive, innovative impact in the world, allowing us to solve some of the toughest problems faced in the life science industry. I am extremely thankful to Hans-Christian Semmler, chairman of the supervisory board of Innoplexus, for being a guiding light for the entire team. He exemplifies relentless pursuit of excellence, at the same time reminding us all that the most important quality for us all is empathy. Hans-Christian has been guiding us to think through to the last detail of any solution. As he always says, "the Devil lies in the details!"

I have been extremely blessed to have received the guidance and mentorship of visionaries, thought leaders, and industry stalwarts from the life science industry. They have been the people who always keep patients and positive impact to society in the center of everything. Dr. Andreas Penk from Pfizer has been a leading light in looking at future trends in the industry and in thinking counterfactually to solve critical problems. I have always benefited immensely from interactions with him. Dr. Stefan Oschmann from Merck KGaA has been looking at the convergence of life science and technology long before others even considered this important. He is one business leader who personifies curiosity. I learned how the right questions can open new opportunities to solve complex problems. Stefan Oelrich from Bayer has been inspirational in terms of marrying future promises of new technology with the pragmatism of today. I have learned from him how to bring the explorational aspects grounded into the exploitative realities of innovation. Similarly, I am thankful to Dr. Hermann Jung, Reto Francioni, Belen Garijo, Udit Batra, Rehan Verjee, Prof. Jochen Maas, Kasper Rorsted, Dr. Alexander Zehnder, Dr. Herbert Mueller, James S. Turley, Dr. Klaus Engel, Florian Rentsch, Prof. Werner Gleissner, Florian Brand, Peter Thiel, Sam Engelbardt, Dan Larimer, and many others for their kind guidance.

Christian Angermayer always reminds me to question the status quo and to have the courage of thinking big. Josef Broich has been the strategist and visionary par excellence. Josef can think through multiple knowledge domains seamlessly and has been a guiding light to leverage ideas from different domains to create impact.

I have learned a lot through my interactions from visionary thinkers such as the late Prof. Sumantra Ghoshal,

Charles Handy, Prof. Daniel Kahneman, and Prof. Philip Kotler. I will always remain grateful to Prof. Florian Taube, Prof. Andreas Eisingerich, and Prof. Nils Stieglitz for being great friends and sounding boards for all my crazy ideas. I am also thankful to Prof. Ronald Gleich, Prof. Asok Misra, Prof. Regina Moczadlo, Prof. Juergen Janovsky, and Prof. Juergen Volkert for their guidance.

I cannot be thankful enough to my mentors and family from EY: Markus Heinen, who has been an inspiration to start this journey, Prof. Michael Schaden, Dr. Hartmut Winkler, Sushiel Keswani, Julie Teigland, Cherie Faiella, and many others. Similarly, mentors and family from BCG: Martin Reeves, who introduced to me the world of mental models and counterfactual rationality, Judith Wallenstein, and Bernd Ziegler, to name a few.

This book has been prepared while leading an AI company in the life sciences, keeping in mind the importance of data in the healthcare industry and how it can be used to save thousands of lives. It has been an exciting time but also one full of many challenges in which I needed continuous motivation and support from my family and friends. First and foremost, I would like to thank my loving wife, Dr. Vidhi Bhardwaj, for keeping up with a crazy schedule of hers and mine. Vidhi was and remains my first advisor when it comes to understanding biological concepts. My parents have always been giving unconditionally, and certainly all good I am blessed with, I owe to them—only my failures are mine. My German family of Krams and Sanyals has always been a constant positive force in my life.

Finally, I dedicate this book to my two beautiful children, Aadya and Vivaan. They constantly teach and remind me of the power of simplicity and curiosity, the two qualities that essentially are also the driving force of life.

ABOUT THE AUTHOR

An Indian-born German citizen, DR. GUNJAN BHARDWAJ holds a doctorate from the European Business School in Germany, an MBA in management and marketing from Pforzheim Graduate School, and a bachelor's from Indian Institute of Technology, Bombay. The founder and CEO of Innoplexus AG, he is the author or coauthor of twenty-three patent applications and has spoken and published worldwide on innovation, artificial intelligence, marketing, and drug development. Gunjan currently serves on multiple advisory boards, including the Centre for Human and Machine Intelligence and the Forbes Technology Council. He lives in Germany.

Printed in Germany
by Amazon Distribution
GmbH, Leipzig

31384136R00075